"This book carries a clear, powerful, and deeply sacred light. A gift to the world." - Bonnie & Brian Winter, Tech Entrepreneurs & Advisors

"Sonya's book beautifully bridges how we are humans living through a spiritual experience. It brings the physical, scientific, and spiritual worlds together like puzzle pieces."
- Ellie Cormier, Heart-Centered Mother and Intuitive

"This transformative work illuminates the spiritual journey with remarkable clarity, guiding readers to develop authentic self-connection through cultivated trust and heightened discernment."
- Angela Bruno, Neuroscientist

"A metaphysical and spiritual powerhouse of wisdom for the modern lightworker. I felt the light while reading it." - Miss Kim, Intuitive Practitioner

"This bright body of work guides readers to recognize their inherent brilliance, reminding us we need not acquire anything more to shine our light." - Amy Allen, Spiritual Advisor

"A master healer who has helped me identify, understand, and release generational trauma. None have helped me heal like Sonya - she is pure magic." - Nora Dobranszky, Doctor of Acupuncture

"In my darkest hours, I found my deepest strength. When I finally awakened, I discovered a love-affirming, consciousness - expanding alignment with the Universe that changed everything. Without a shadow of doubt, Sonya Lee doesn't just teach about channeling light - she embodies it completely."
- Jonathan Brambles, Chief Marketing Officer

CHANNELS
OF LIGHT

CHANNELS OF LIGHT

Awakening Your Divine Purpose
in a World That Needs Your Light

Sonya Lee

Channels of Light: Awakening Your Divine Purpose in a World That Needs Your Light

Published by Quantum Leader Press
Idyllwild, California, U.S.A.
Copyright ©2025, Sonya Lee. All rights reserved.

No part of this book may be reproduced in any form or by any mechanical means, including information storage and retrieval systems without permission in writing from the publisher/author, except by a reviewer who may quote passages in a review. All images, logos, quotes, and trademarks included in this book are subject to use according to trademark and copyright laws of the United States of America.

Lee, Sonya, Author
CHANNELS OF LIGHT
Sonya Lee

Library of Congress Control Number: 2025907367

ISBN: 979-8-9985470-0-3, 979-8-9985470-2-7 (paperback)
ISBN: 979-8-9985470-3-4 (hardcover)
ISBN: 979-8-9985470-1-0 (digital)
ISBN: 979-8-9985470-4-1 (audio)

BODY, MIND & SPIRIT / Inspiration & Personal Growth
PHILOSOPHY / Metaphysics
HEALTH & FITNESS / Alternative Therapies
BODY, MIND & SPIRIT / Gaia & Earth Energies

Book Design: Sonya Lee, sonyalee.io
Author Photo: Cierra Breeze, cierrabreeze.com
Publishing Management: Susie Schaefer, finishthebookpublishing.com

QUANTITY PURCHASES: Schools, companies, professional groups, clubs, and other organizations may qualify for special terms when ordering quantities of this title. For information, email contact@sonyalee.io

All rights reserved by Sonya Lee and Quantum Leader Press.
This book is printed in the United States of America.

DEDICATION

To modern-day humans who are awakening to the simple pleasures of joy, peace, and compassion - you don't have to change who you are except to be more authentic than ever.

CONTENTS

0, Introduction: Awakening the Channel of Light Within You	1
1, The Universe Within: Foundations of Cosmic Energy	11
2, Our Cosmic Origins: Beyond Earthly Understanding	21
3, Consciousness Unbound: The Quantum Perspective	33
4, Deprogramming the Subconscious: Breaking Karmic Patterns	45
5, The Hierarchy of Spiritual Guidance	57
6, Awakening Intuition and Channeling Mastery	71
7, Meditation: The Gateway to Inner Realms	87
8, Holistic Health and Energy Healing	103
9, Sacred Geometry and Universal Patterns	119
10, Stories of Transformation and Awakening	129
11, Integration of Science and Spirituality	145
12, Ethical Living and Universal Responsibility	155
13, Navigating Spiritual Challenges and Dark Nights of the Soul	173
14, Establishing Healthy Boundaries in Spiritual Practice	187
15, Becoming a Channel of Light Here on Earth	205
Continuing Your Journey: Resources and Practices	219
Appendix	229
Bonus: Experience the Power of a Quantum Meditation	241
Acknowledgments	247
About the Author	253

FOREWORD

My friend Sonya is the wisest and kindest soul I know. Let this book inspire us to understand the world and ourselves more deeply. It gives us the courage to confront our darkness, transforming it into understanding and allowing us to share our love and purpose with the world, just as Sonya does.

Her authenticity is so profound that her presence creates a shift in energy wherever she goes. I see so many people these days searching for real answers, tired of all the fake spirituality out there. Sonya's book arrives exactly when we needed it most. This isn't just another spiritual book filled with nice quotes - it's a genuine guide on how to live with deeper wisdom in our chaotic modern world.

I am so happy she wrote this wonderful book, which allows us to learn from her experiences and gain greater knowledge about the possibilities and endless wonders of life.

Months ago, if you had asked me about energy and light, I would have given you a simple answer without much experience or understanding of the terms or sensations they can create. But when Sonya entered my life in divine timing, she became the teacher I needed to survive what she kindly calls a "rude awakening." You could also describe it as a manic phase and a transformation in my understanding of myself and the world around me.

What sets Sonya apart from other teachers I've met is her ability to access incredible spiritual realms while still communicating like an ordinary person about everyday matters. She doesn't hide behind complicated spiritual jargon - she simply shows you how to apply this wisdom to real-life situations, whether you're dealing with work stress or relationship challenges.

I'll never forget our first session.

So much was happening that I knew something was going to shift, but never in a million years did I think my mind could grasp and embrace this new and wonderful reality that Sonya helped me accept.

She pulled some oracle cards and asked, "Are you sleeping a lot? It's time to rest - you'll need it."

At that time, I was indeed sleeping for hours each night and even more during the day. How could she possibly know that two weeks later, I would enter a phase of minimal - or sometimes no - sleep at all, which lasted for a good two months? She foresaw so much of what would unfold in the coming weeks and months - separations, realizations, diagnoses - and she guided me through months of serious emotional turmoil.

As someone who deals with high-pressure situations myself, I love how Sonya blends spiritual understanding with practical advice. Her years of working with major companies mean she understands what it's like to live in the real world. Even my most skeptical friends are surprised by how much sense her explanations make.

My emotions were so intense that I clung to life while enduring pain and confusion to the point where my mind lost its ability to make sense of the world around me. All I could do was try to make sense of myself. I lost my mind for months, and yet she held space for me. More than that, she taught me everything I needed to know about energy, light, darkness, realities, dimensions, souls, angels, God, and the Universe - concepts I had never fully understood or even believed in before. She taught me about the world as it truly is.

Having worked with various healers throughout my journey, I can honestly say that Sonya's abilities are unlike any others I've encountered. Her forensic approach to energy healing - tracing issues across timelines and dimensions - helped me heal things I didn't know could be healed. When nothing else worked, Sonya's methods did.

She was the flashlight guiding me through darkness so I could reclaim my light. I am humbled to have met Sonya at such a crucial time in my life because I cannot deny that she was divinely placed there to help me save myself and transition into a deeper understanding of my spiritual being.

This book isn't just something to read - it's something to experience. As you move through its pages, you'll feel the same energy and light that Sonya brings to her sessions. The wisdom she shares here isn't just interesting - it's essential for navigating the intense changes happening in our world right now.

I feel grateful that she entered my life and shared so much of her wisdom with me. I am constantly amazed by her ability to flow through dimensions, feel energy, and translate it in ways that simplify life's complexity for me. Every day, I continue to be inspired by her presence, love, generosity, and being. This book is yet another gift from her - a gift that keeps on giving - and I feel deeply thankful to be in her orbit. Her wisdom has the power to change lives; it certainly saved mine.

Maya Gabeira
Brazilian Surfer, 2x World Record Holder
Author and Activist

Introduction: Awakening the Channel of Light Within You

Do you feel like you don't really fit or belong in this world? As if you are holding a deeper purpose within you beyond your day job, career, or the roles you've assumed based on where life has taken you? Do you ever find yourself gazing up at the stars, feeling a connection to something unexplainably greater, but you can't quite put your finger on it?

If so, this book was written for you.

You are probably wondering - what is a "Channel of Light"?

A channel of light is someone who creates space within themselves for a higher power - whether it's God, the Universe, Source, Spirit, or Creator - allowing this power to flow through you in your words, actions, and presence.

Think of it this way. Just as a physical water pipe creates a pathway through which water can flow from one location to another, a human channel allows wisdom, healing, light, inspiration, love, and joy to flow freely from an invisible realm into our daily lives.

Being a channel of light doesn't mean you need to be completely perfect or free from mistakes or misgivings. If anything, it means that you allow your true nature to shine brightly into the world you live in. It means that you also understand you are not separate from a higher power, but rather that you allow that higher power to be expressed through your personality, skills, gifts, and even your weaknesses.

A light channel connects directly with the Universe to communicate, share, and express unconditional beauty in a myriad of ways. Some do this through healing work, while others do it through music or creating art. Some share light through leadership, teaching, parenting, or simply bringing warmth and wisdom into everyday conversations. There is no specific way to be a channel, except for you to be the most authentic version of yourself.

Perhaps above all, being a channel of light means that your life has greater meaning and purpose. When you feel that you are meant for and aligned with something greater than regular life, beyond your job description, it means that your soul is finally answering its calling. As you begin to see yourself as a channel for profound truth to flow through you, your daily activities take on greater meaning.

You begin to realize that your existence here on earth does make a difference, even if your unique combination of life experiences, gifts, and even scars do not make sense to you. Your unique combination qualifies you to be a channel of light in your own distinct way, to serve in ways that others are not qualified to do.

The idea of a channel of light came to me when I was a young child. At that time, I lacked the vocabulary to explain this feeling of being part of something larger than myself. Like many of us, I put this feeling aside for decades as I navigated the everyday realities of school, maturation, and career development.

I spent twenty-five years in the corporate world as a business consultant to Fortune 100 companies. Over time, I honed my craft in the business world, becoming skilled in business analysis, strategy, organizational dynamics, branding, and marketing. I knew how to work with high-powered executives and build high-performance teams, rising in the ranks of professional accomplishments. Despite taking a twenty-five-year detour, this part of my life now makes sense. It wasn't a sidetrack from my spiritual path today; rather, it served as a training ground that allowed me to bring a distinctive perspective and credibility to how I teach and guide spiritual knowledge in everyday life.

My business background has trained me well to navigate complex situations, taught me how to lead people and organizations through significant transformations, and shown me how to maintain perspective under stress - all practical skills that have served me well in my spiritual work. During my business years, I felt that I had abandoned my purpose. But now, I can see that this was actually guiding me to my divine destiny - to bridge the gap between a professional world and a spiritual path. The journey from the boardroom to spiritual practice has finally come full circle, and now I'm able to speak both languages.

I am, after all, the daughter and granddaughter of medicine healers and shamans. Not business tycoons or strategists.

It's strange for me to say this, but as stubborn as I am, it took a devastating personal crisis to fully shake me up and awaken my role as a channel of light.

During a particularly low point in my life that was extremely depressive and difficult, I questioned everything. I am ashamed to admit that I did not have the energy to keep on living and was fighting off dark thoughts on a regular basis. As I began to heal and slowly recover, I turned to a higher power and gave up on the idea of controlling the outcome of my life. My own life experiences of being raised in a Buddhist monastery as a child and abandoned by my family had to serve a greater purpose...

One particular morning, asleep in my one-bedroom apartment in Huntington Beach, CA, I awoke to an unforgettable view - seventeen of my deceased ancestors huddled in the corner of my bedroom staring at me with great worry. Standing at the very front, as if posing for a group photo, were my maternal grandmother and grandfather. I saw other people standing to their left and right, recognizing them as ancestors I had never seen or met during life. Frozen in shock, I counted all of them and filed their faces into my memory.

Unable to manage my emotions, I stared at the vision a little longer and noticed a woman standing at the very back. She was dressed in a traditional Chinese headdress from the dynasties and a formal dark, dress-like uniform. She stared at me with compassionate eyes as I realized she was pleading with me to heal myself with great compassion. With tears streaming down my face and confusion that I was having a depressive episode, I slowly returned to my pillow and fell back asleep with even more tears in my eyes. I could not handle what I was witnessing.

When I finally woke up, I got dressed and left my apartment in a hurry. I simply could not bear to manage the sight of seventeen ancestors gravely watching over me. Later that day, I called my best friend, Tamara, who suggested that I ask my grandfather telepathically why they were visiting me. He replied:

"We are here because we are extremely worried about you, Sanya."

"Why me?" I asked.

"Because you are the last of our lineage. We need you to continue the work. If not you, all will be lost. You are the only one who can continue on behalf of our entire family and dynasty."

It took me many months to come to terms with these words.

Every time I recall this conversation, a lump forms in my throat, as I now understand why I had to go through what I did. This led me to a path of discovery that would ultimately change my life direction and sense of purpose. Many years later, through research and deep spiritual meditation, I would come to understand that the woman in the back of the vision was a shaman priestess from the Shang Dynasty (c. 1600 - c. 1046 BCE) - a time when emperors had a court of male and female shamans who served as bridges between the human and spirit realms.

What surprised me the most is that my psychic abilities, which had unfolded without formal training or guidance from any mentors, mirrored those of my ancient ancestor. I understood that her skill set were mine. But more importantly, that she was me. I am her. In some way, across centuries and through many generations, I had reconnected with the ability to channel wisdom, facilitate healing, and communicate with realms invisible to most. The only difference is that today, I am meant to serve as a spiritual facilitator in ways that help regular people connect and integrate spiritual wisdom into their everyday practice.

I survived my pain. I survived my desire to leave this world. My personal crisis made me realize that I can transform the energy of pain and suffering into profound meaning. This helped me to understand what it means to truly be a channel of light.

When we live as a channel of light, we:
- Endeavor to be the most sincere, purposeful, and powerful version of ourselves.
- Share healing, wisdom, and love with others
- Connect our existence here on earth with a greater power
- Help others recognize their own goodness and purpose
- Make the world a little brighter with our service and presence
- Share universal truths using our own authentic nature
- Develop spiritual awareness in our ordinary, everyday activities

I am frequently amazed by my own spiritual gifts, marveling at how I can possibly know what I haven't learned. And then it dawned on me that perhaps my soul volunteered to come back to this timeline once again to help the world become a better place.

The call of my ancestors to carry on our lineage initially felt overwhelming, causing unnecessary expectations and responsibilities. But as I sat with this understanding and a higher truth, I now know that I am here to shine as bright as possible, in my own way, having overcome my many challenging life experiences, to build the strength to shine the way for others.

Let me be clear - being a channel of light is not reserved for unique individuals who are born with special abilities. It is meant for each one of us in our most natural and authentic state - to become the version of us that accepts every aspect of who we are, even the good, bad, and ugly. Being a channel of light is the opposite of pretentious spirituality. The concept of being a channel of light thrives on your most authentic nature.

All of us are light channels at the very core, however, many of us have forgotten this reality. Waking up to this awareness is not about becoming enlightened; it's about remembering who you've always been, deep down in your soul's truth, and giving yourself permission to radiate authenticity in the way you live and interact with others, right now, not later.

I wrote this book to share all the things I've learned along the way - not because I have all the answers, but because I truly want to help you find and expand on your own unique way of expressing life as your own channel of light.

My spiritual belief system consists of 'all of the above,' in reverence for the respect I have for many great religions and belief systems. I believe that each spiritual tradition offers valuable wisdom and insights into the human experience and our connection to the divine. I honor the personal lessons and inner truths that resonate with each individual soul, regardless of their chosen path.

While I may frequently use Christian language in this book, such as Jesus, God, Mother Mary, Archangels, and other figures, this choice stems from practical considerations rather than religious exclusivity. These names and archetypes serve as accessible reference points for discussing specific frequencies and vibrational qualities that transcend any single tradition. They act as a common language - a universal spiritual vocabulary that many people can relate to regardless of their background.

For instance, when I speak of Archangel Michael, I'm referring to a specific energetic frequency of protection and truth. When I mention Mother Mary, I'm invoking the universal qualities of compassion and divine feminine nurturing. These beings represent archetypal energies that appear across cultures under different names and forms.

I deeply respect the foundational principles and teachings that guide each person forward on their spiritual journey. Whether someone connects with Buddhist mindfulness, Hindu concepts of karma, Islamic devotion, Jewish mysticism, Indigenous wisdom traditions, or any other path, I recognize the divine spark within each of these approaches. My inclusive perspective allows me to work with people from all backgrounds, meeting them where they are while honoring the unique spiritual framework that resonates with their soul.

Whether you are just starting to dig deeper into your spiritual practice or have been walking a path of personal development and growth, these pages hold practical advice for becoming a clearer and brighter channel for the light that already exists within you.

The world is hungry for what you have to offer - your own unique expression of universal light and truth that connects us all in humanity.

As you step into your path of becoming your own authentic channel of light, you also create a ripple effect that is far beyond what can be measured or noticed. Each person that you interact with becomes a little bit brighter, awakening the hearts of countless others. This world will bring about a shift in the collective consciousness of our world - something we are all hungry for.

In this book, I'll share my own stories, practical methods, and timeless wisdom for navigating the joys and challenges of life. We will learn how to trust the highest guidance, develop our intuitive abilities, balance the energies, and radiate our light in a way that serves our highest purpose for the greater good. I have deliberately omitted mentioning specific people in my life as a way to protect our privacy; know that this is not to ignore or pretend they do not exist.

My most sincere hope is that these pages will help you to realize the light that you already are and serve as a guide for letting that light shine more brightly into every aspect of your life. For in becoming a channel of light, you don't become something different from who you are - you simply let go of the blocks and obstacles that prevent you from expressing who you've always been at your core.
This path of actualization and expression is not always comfortable, yet it is immeasurably rewarding.

And you are not journeying this path all by yourself.

Many others are also waking up, forming a web of light that becomes more powerful with each individual who remembers their most authentic self and purpose. I hope you will have as much pleasure reading this book as I have had writing it. May it be both lamp and mirror - reflecting to you the light that is already within you and lighting the way as you step more fully into your role as a channel of light. This world needs your unique perspective more than ever.

In gratitude and love to your light,
Sonya

Chapter 1: The Universe Within: Foundations of Cosmic Energy

The sweet scent of sandalwood incense carries me back to my grandmother's small temple in Hong Kong in the 1980s. I was eight years old when my family moved across the ocean, leaving behind the familiar Canadian landscapes for a world that would reshape my understanding of existence itself.

Sitting on small wooden stools, my grandmother and I would spend time in her converted one-bedroom apartment. The living room had become home to a giant altar, where dozens of Buddha statues, deities, and enlightened beings watched over us - the compassionate Kwan Yin, the enlightened Buddha, the eccentric Ji Gong, the loyal Kuan Gong, and the ancestral spirits who blessed our lineage.

I loved my grandmother the most. I loved holding her hands, tracing the deep lines on her palms with my small fingers.

"Every line tells a story," she would say, her eyes sparkling with wisdom as she let me explore the roadmap of her life written in her skin.

She always knew what to say. When my stomach hurt from too many street snacks or when my temper kept me awake, she would place her warm, soft, pudgy hands on my belly, humming healing sounds that vibrated through my entire being. The pain would always slowly fade away, whether from her healing energy or simply the comfort of her presence - I will never know.

Those five years in Hong Kong, from the age of eight to thirteen, allowed me to experience some sense of normalcy in my life. I went to a private international school, but spent many of our family weekends at my grandmother's temple. Many of her teachings were beyond what I could grasp at that time, but I remember every feeling and absorbed as many mysterious lessons as I could grasp.

"Watch the incense smoke, San-ya," she would say to me in Cantonese, drawing my attention to the delicate plume rising from the altar. "See how straight it rises? That means that the connection with the Heavens is strong and clear today."

On other days, when the smoke coiled and danced in spiral patterns, she would smile at me knowingly. "Ah, the Gods above are listening closely to our prayers now." I would watch, mesmerized, as the smoke created ethereal patterns in the air, each shape holding meaning that my grandmother could interpret like a sacred text.

In those early years, my grandmother taught me that energy wasn't just an abstract concept - it was something you could feel, touch, and even see if you knew how to look for it. She would task me with lighting incense, but also guide me to sense the subtle differences in energy at home, school, in my heart, with friends, family, and more.

"Close your eyes," she would instruct, "and feel the energy flowing through you."

Through practice, I learned to distinguish the warmth of my own body from the divine feminine presence of Kwan Yin, though I couldn't explain how I knew.

"Everything is connected," she would say, taking my hands in hers and pressing our palms together. "Can you feel how the energy is buzzing between us? It's the same life force that flows through the trees, the mountains, and even the stars."

When the adults were deep in ceremony, I would stand off to the side and watch them. Someone - usually my mother or father - would divinate information using a makeshift rod and write Chinese characters in a flat table of sand. When I asked what they were doing, they would explain that they were asking the Gods above for medicine scripts.

"It's to help them get better, San-Ya", my grandmother would say. I'd nod in agreement, not quite understanding their magic.

Sometimes, when I had a tummy ache, my grandmother would rub her hands on my stomach and explain how those aches are related to different parts of our body because of our emotions and spirit. I didn't understand all the terminologies then, but I could feel that warmth as she taught me - what I would eventually discover were some of the body's meridian systems, which are simply channels where life energy passes through.

Her small temple wasn't large, but it felt infinite. Every corner held mysteries, every altar statue emanated its unique presence, and the air itself seemed alive with possibilities. The chanting of prayers, the gentle ring of brass bells, and the continuous curl of incense smoke created an atmosphere where the boundary between the physical and spiritual worlds became wonderfully blurred.

At the age of thirteen, my path led me to a traditional Buddhist monastery in the United States, across the world from my family. Though my mother's decision came from a deep calling to a spiritual truth, the separation from my parents - and my beloved grandparents - was absolutely heart-wrenching.

The monastery's stone-cold walls and strict routines were a big difference from the warmth of my grandmother's embrace. Yet, it was here, in the midst of both profound spiritual discovery and intense personal challenges, that the seeds of wisdom my grandmother had planted began to bloom.

At the monastery, elementary school classes brought new depth to my grandmother's wisdom. The senior nuns taught us children what I had intuitively picked up, creating a blueprint that helped me understand more mystical experiences. They taught us that the Buddha-nature, or consciousness itself, is a form of energy that is capable of transforming both our inner and outer worlds. We do so through intense prayer and meditation.

During long meditation sessions in the grand Buddha hall or late at night in the girls' dormitory, my mind would often wander back home to my friends, classmates, parents, and grandparents in Hong Kong. I missed them all. I was so naive at that time. Thinking that they would realize their honest mistake and come and take me home. But, they didn't. I cried for two weeks straight. I lost my voice and was bedridden. I could barely eat any food. I didn't want to drink any water. Despite my friends trying to cheer me up, I could not help but feel depressed and abandoned. We were all stuck at the monastery, together.

With time, my heart slowly healed. The monks and nuns at the monastery instructed us to pay attention to our thoughts, intentions, and actions. Every thought, they said, has its own energetic signature that ripples into our personal energy field, which reaches far beyond our physical boundaries. Once a week, on weekends, the girls' dormitory students would gather in a circle and share what they had observed about themselves that week. After each share, we would open the floor for discussion, to agree or disagree on whether we were good or not, holding each other to a much higher standard of living and breathing. The practice of mindful awareness eventually formed the basis of my spiritual growth.

Through hours of meditation and mindfulness, I learned to sense and feel incredibly subtle energies or shifts. The monastery itself had a complicated history - what I would call "haunted." Not quite the scary type of haunting you find in films, but more the residual energetic imprint of people who had lived there before. There were spots throughout the 700 acres of land that felt weighted with residual sadness, and others that rang with joy or peace. It was mostly sadness, however. With increasing energetic sensitivity, I could often feel the different energies around me as distinctly as changes in temperature or texture in the air.

Some nights, I would hear faint whispers in empty hallways or catch glimpses of shadowy, dark figures that would disappear when I turned to look directly. The older nuns matter-of-factly acknowledged these ghostly presences, teaching us not to fear them but to understand them as part of our earthly existence, souls still attached to the physical plane for various reasons. They taught us how to have compassion for these spirits, helping them find peace while maintaining our energetic boundaries.

I remember a time when the girls gathered on a Sunday for an arts and crafts project. The nuns had found some fabric and gave us the option to cut and sew it into objects of our choice. Sensing the fabric, I knew it wasn't meant for me (or us) to touch, so I kindly declined the invitation. Later that night, I mysteriously woke up around 2 am to feel a spirit wandering through the dormitory. I could sense that it was visiting specific children - those who had touched and played with the cloth. When I finally found the courage to open my eyes, I saw a dark figure in the shape of a human. The minute the spirit became aware of me, it faded into nothingness. These experiences were just everyday occurrences in my childhood.

As time went on, not only did I learn to sense spirits, but I also learned how different thought patterns and emotions could create various types of energy inside and around me. I had grown increasingly comfortable with the unseen world around us, but there wasn't really a choice not to see them.

During the years I was separated from my family, the cold walls and teachings from the monks and nuns became both a comfort and a tool for healing. I was deeply fascinated with the paranormal and learned that even across space and time, the energetic bonds of love and connection can remain unbroken. The pain I experienced from our separation gradually turned into a deeper appreciation for the invisible threads that connect us all.

The monastery's teachings expanded on what my grandmother had taught me about humans being imperfect yet perfect microcosms of the Universe. The monks and nuns also taught us children the short and long-form movements of Tai Chi Chuan to help us understand the flow of energy within my own body. Each move, thought, and action contributes to our physical, emotional, and spiritual well-being.

I would rub my belly now and again, like my grandmother had taught me, re-experiencing once more her warm and secure feeling of safety and love. By now, I had learned that my emotions, especially grief, were connected to an invisible network of energy points - channels through which life energy (known as "chi" or "qi" in Chinese modalities) flows through our bodies.

These energy points, invisible but noticeable to the trained touch, connect our organs, nervous system, and spiritual truths about our purpose in a web that is beyond what is commonly recognized by Western practices. Energy flows between these energy points along specific meridians in the body. When these energetic 'streams' flow freely, there is health and abundance. When they are restricted by tension or emotional blocks, there can be discomfort and dis-ease. My grandmother's healing touch was based on the understanding that energy can also be released, diverted, or healed.

I learned that when we bottle up our emotions and don't express them, it can affect our entire physical and mental being, as I learned firsthand in my bouts of homesickness and pent-up anger.

At a young age, I also learned about the ancient system of chakras. Chakras provide a framework for understanding how energy is stored in the body and moves through us. There are seven main chakra points, starting from the base of our spine and leading all the way to the top of our head. Each chakra governs and represents a different aspect of our human experience:

The Root Chakra is located at the base of the spine in the pelvic area. This center controls safety, stability, and our basic human needs. When healthy, we walk the world with confidence and power. When blocked, there may be fear - a fear of survival or being constantly uprooted. To understand how this chakra affects your life, examine your relationships with money, food, and safety in the world.

The Sacral Chakra is in the lower abdomen, just three inches below the belly. This delicate point governs our emotional world, personal pleasure, and relationships. When balanced, we easily adapt to life's changes with grace and can express ourselves freely. When imbalanced, emotional extremes or creative blocks can arise. This chakra's condition reflects our capacity for joy and our ability to maintain healthy boundaries.

The Solar Plexus Chakra is located in the upper abdomen. It governs our center of personal power, authentic purpose, career, identity, self-worth, and will power. Balance in this chakra brings confidence and authority. Any blockages can manifest as self-doubt or control issues. Watch how you present yourself in professional settings or make personal decisions - this chakra represents your career, identity, and life purpose. When I work with clients who want to know about their purpose, I often tap into this point for answers.

The Heart Chakra - our largest energy point is located at the center of the chest. This chakra connects our physical and spiritual selves through compassionate love. More than just romantic love, this center governs our ability to develop relationships and have empathy for ourselves and others. An open heart creates a greater capacity for deep connection and inner peace. When closed, isolation and fear of intimacy may follow. Our most meaningful connections flow from this powerful place.

The Throat Chakra is related to expressing our truth. It governs all forms of expression. When this chakra is balanced and open, I can sense clear communication and effective listening. When blocked, we might struggle to speak our needs or share our gifts. This chakra's health reflects our conversations, creative pursuits, and ability to advocate for ourselves.

The Third Eye is the soft spot between the eyebrows. This center governs intuition, perception, and imagination. When this invisible eye is open, we trust our intuition and see beyond physical limitations. Imbalance might appear as a spiritual disconnection or over-reliance on logic at the expense of our intuitive knowing. Our ability to imagine limitless possibilities beyond our current circumstances flows from this mystical center.

The Crown Chakra, a thousand-petaled lotus, is located at the top of the head. This highest chakra connects us to a divine universal consciousness and our infinite wisdom. Balance in this chakra brings a profound sense of purpose and spiritual connection. When blocked, meaninglessness and isolation may cloud our days. When fully open, we can access the wisdom of the vast Universe and trust that we are divinely guided and protected.

I work with the chakras regularly with my clients, allowing me to pinpoint areas of concern immediately, rather than waiting months, years, or decades to understand what troubles them.

The monastery has undoubtedly influenced who I am today. Now, after spending twenty-five years in the corporate world, away from my formal spiritual practice, I've come full circle, returning to the wisdom and traditions that shaped my early years. The trauma of separation from my family has finally healed through patience, empathy, and understanding that we are never truly separate - we are all interconnected through the vast web of universal energy and truth.

Today, when I close my eyes in meditation, I can still feel my grandmother's presence around me. I can sense the unique quality of silence in her temple, and smell the sweet sandalwood incense rising to the heavens. When I miss her, I simply close my eyes and connect to her energy. I can talk to her directly as my spirit guide. Even though my past isn't full of fond memories, it is full of energetic imprints that have shaped who I am and how I understand the Universe today.

Through understanding all of the changing seasons in life, this truth remains: We are all channels of light, unique and authentic expressions of universal energy.

The practices and understandings I gained, first through my grandmother's loving guidance and later through my monastic upbringing, have finally merged, allowing me to help others recognize and work with their inner truth and light. Each one of us carries the same energy that flows through stars and galaxies.

As we learn to recognize this truth about energy, we become

conscious participants in a world of creation. Every day, we create through our very existence. Whether sitting in meditation or moving through our busy daily lives, we can learn to feel and flow with the wisdom that exists deep in our soul.

The Universe that exists within each of us opens us up to infinite potential. Energy flows where our attention goes. When we learn to direct our attention skillfully, we become channels for transformation and healing—not just for ourselves, but for all the lives we encounter and touch.

> *"In the great dance of cosmic energy,*
> *we are both the dancers and the dance itself."*

Chapter 2: Our Cosmic Origins: Beyond Earthly Understanding

My spiritual education in Hong Kong wasn't just limited to my grandmother. While my family spent weekends at the temple, our evenings often involved rushing home to watch recorded VHS documentaries about aliens, UFOs, and extraterrestrial life. My father introduced me to these types of documentaries, creating a different kind of education.

"What do you think this is about?" my father would ask. He'd press the pause button on the remote control as I stared intensely at the television screen, donning images of little grey aliens. As an engineer, he approached these topics with genuine scientific curiosity.

"I'm not sure," I'd reply, considering the evidence presented. "But, I believe in energy and spirits. Could they be connected? We are not alone in this world, right?"

We would carefully record these programs, creating a library of cosmic possibilities that we would revisit and discuss on weekends. My father would explore and explain various theories about enlightenment, humanity's cosmic origins, old Chinese myths, and healing modalities with the same precision he applied to his professional work.

It's important to note that my father is also a Feng Shui master and a Master Numerologist, in addition to being a Civil Engineer for the

Hong Kong Government. I loved being able to use spiritual logic in these conversations.

The exploration of ancient wisdom and paranormal curiosities shaped my understanding of human existence and consciousness in the greater Universe. Little did I know, at that time, that these early experiences were actually preparing me for a much deeper journey into the nature of existence itself.

During my years at the Buddhist monastery, I began to experience phenomena that didn't exactly fit into traditional teachings.

When the lights went out at night, I would often sense, feel, or see presences around me - not the ancestral spirits I had learned about from my grandmother, but something different from other realms of existence. Though I hadn't yet developed my gifts of clairvoyance, these experiences planted seeds of understanding that would make sense many decades later.

Even in those early years, I carried a deep, inexplicable knowing that I was meant to help people. I distinctly remember crying hysterically, by myself, that I was not yet ready to die. I was only 11 years old and had no concept of death yet.

My desire wasn't a career goal or a desire to be altruistic for people-pleasing purposes - it was a soul-level certainty that felt as if it had been encoded into the very fiber of my existence. I couldn't articulate what this meant or how it would happen, but the feeling was strong enough to keep me committed to understanding life and beyond.

As I grew older, this certainty began to take on a more definite form. In my twenties, I started experiencing what I would later understand as channeling, though at the time, I had no framework to understand what was happening. Information and insights would flow into and through me, seemingly out of nowhere, offering perspectives and understanding that felt both foreign and deeply familiar.

"Hey, Wendy, did you just cut your pinky?"

"Uhh... how did you know?" my University roommate asked after I felt a sharp pain in my pinky finger. She and I sat in our dorm room with our backs facing each other. There was no way for me to have seen it happen.

"I... I'm not sure," I admitted. "I just felt a cut on my finger and thought I would ask you." There was no logical explanation for how I would have known (and for her to confirm) that she had indeed gotten a paper cut.

It was as if some part of me had access to an intricate library of knowledge beyond books, but my conscious mind wasn't quite ready to accept what was happening.

In my thirties, I became obsessed with my career at Warner Bros. and later Disney. I invested a great deal of time in my non-profit animal rescue, the Santé D'Or Foundation, where my co-founders and I applied holistic and intuitive care to the cats, dogs, and rabbits we rescued from high-kill shelters. In addition to animal rescue, we offered healing services to the local Los Feliz, California, community, including animal communication, healing touch, and Bach flower remedies.

My corporate life has exposed me to a world of strategic thinking and complex problem-solving. I worked as an award-winning designer with major entertainment brands and eventually consulted for Fortune 100 companies, including Skechers, Cisco, and eBay. My favorite project to date will always be the official Warner Bros. Harry Potter movie website. What's fascinating, in hindsight, is how these seemingly separate and distinct paths were actually converging – the analytical frameworks I created for business challenges were also unknowingly preparing me to structure and translate spiritual concepts in a way that people could understand.

By my forties, things started to make more sense. My spiritual practice had evolved into active channeling with angels and archangels. I started to integrate the wisdom from the Universe and beings from the stars by speaking directly to higher powers up there.

The engineer's daughter, who had watched UFO documentaries with wide-eyed wonder, now understood that the truth of our cosmic existence is far more profound than alien visitations or top-secret marvels. Beyond that, I learned how to see and move energy. It was a truly fascinating time in my life.

Consider this: We, in our human forms, are actually aliens, temporarily dropped into physical bodies.

If you are open to this idea, perhaps you can extend the thought that our souls are fragments of the Universe, in a form of light and energy, choosing to experience Earth in a physical form as a giant experiment called 'Life School'.

Whether you believe that or not, can we agree that we are not just human beings having an occasional spiritual experience - we are spiritual beings deliberately choosing to have a human experience? There is so much to learn here in this world.

Each of us is born into the world at a particular time, in a specific location, to specific parents, in a specific environment, and a particular era. Perhaps these aren't random circumstances, but strategically planned conditions designed to support the soul's journey of growth and contribution. Is that possible?

Imagine that life is just but a theatrical play.

Each soul chooses to come to Earth, to play specific roles, to explore particular experiences, to contribute to each other's lives, to understand and explore what life could be like under any circumstance.

Some roles that we play in others' lives can bring joy, pain, and everything in between. Still, all are designed to contribute to a more powerful collective experience that helps a collective consciousness (known as the Universe) evolve and expand.

What if the Universe is constantly evolving, wanting to try and experience with the many permutations of life, to build a greater library of understanding and awareness?

I'd like to believe that the international school in Hong Kong where I bounced between Eastern and Western worldviews, the weekends spent absorbing ancient wisdom at my grandmother's temple, the evenings analyzing paranormal phenomena with my father - all these experiences including the years at the monastery were precisely designed for my soul's journey so that I could be right here, right now, with you - helping you become a channel of light.

The thing is, Earth holds a very powerful and unique position in the greater cosmic ecosystem.

We, as human beings, are what I've come to understand as 'creator beings'. A creator being is a soul who has explicitly chosen to incarnate into physical form to specifically work with matter, to shape, imagine, and create in ways that pure photonic energy cannot. To make things a bit more clear, I will use the word 'being' to describe a life form, existence, or aliens. If an energy being can exist as pure energetic consciousness in the great Universe, then we humans have the unique advantage of bridging the physical and spiritual realms to manifest and transform energy into form through our thoughts, actions, and intentions. Being a 'creator being' means that we can create Heaven here on Earth.

If plausible, this helps explain why Earth seems to be such a crucial part of the universe's growth and transformation.

The very challenges that make our human existence difficult - the density of physical matter, the limitations of time and space, the veil that blinds us from our spiritual awareness - are precisely what make it such a powerful environment for soul evolution.

"Sometimes I wonder why life has to be so hard," a client once told me during a session.

"The resistance in life that you feel is just like the resistance a weightlifter needs to build strength," I explained. "Our souls choose to come to Earth precisely because of - not despite - its challenges."

As a 'creator being', we can eat, sleep, play, talk, sing, laugh, dance, paint, draw, and a whole slew of things that an energy form can not do. How powerful is that?

This leads me back to my original point - the pain I felt being separated from my family during my monastery years, the confusion of seeing and feeling spirits without understanding what was happening, the long journey of discovering and accepting my ability to do psychic things - all of these experiences were part of my soul's chosen curriculum. All of my experiences were carefully selected opportunities for growth and understanding. This is why some people refer to Earth as 'Life School'.

There are so many people who do not feel like they are from Earth. Many of my clients feel like they're from the stars, often feeling confused and lost. I've come to understand that many of us here on Earth, including myself, are what we call starseeds - a term that may be new to some readers.

Let me try to explain this to you. Starseeds are beings whose existence and life go back to other star systems, dimensions, and realities in the Universe rather than Earth itself. Just as a plant grows from the specific seed that determines its nature, starseeds carry the energetic imprint of their cosmic home.

Let's imagine that souls can originate from different parts of the Universe, each carrying unique energetic signatures and qualities. Just as a person born in China might carry cultural influences different from someone born in Brazil, souls that originate from different star systems carry distinct cosmic influences. These cosmic influences can shape their perspectives, abilities, and the lessons they're here to learn and teach.

Starseeds often experience life on Earth as if they're visitors or transplants. They may feel a persistent homesickness for a place they can't name, experience recurring dreams of star systems, or civilizations they've never seen in this lifetime, or possess innate knowledge of cosmic principles without having any formal education in these areas. Many starseeds have an intense fascination with the Universe and outer space from early childhood. They feel a sense of familiarity when learning about certain star systems, such as the Pleiades, Sirius, or Arcturus. Just because you aren't from Earth does not mean that you're different or wrong - actually, quite the opposite. If you can understand that your cosmic or soul origin is from somewhere beyond Earth, this can also help you recognize that we are all connected on Earth, as an energy form, for a similar reason.

Starseeds often carry a deep sense of mission, a feeling of being different, and an inexplicable knowing that they're here to contribute to humanity's evolution. The undefined certainty I felt as a child about helping others was my starseed nature already making itself known, long before I had the context to understand it.

"I've always felt like I am not from here," people often tell me during sessions.

"I can relate. That feeling isn't wrong," I responded. "Your soul is trying to get you to remember who you are and why you are here. You've done most of the human things you are expected to do, and now it's time to return to your spiritual truths."

The feeling of being somehow different, of not quite fitting into conventional expectations or structures, is common among starseeds. Some people find themselves drawn to multiple spiritual traditions without fully resonating with any one in particular. Others discover they have natural healing abilities, heightened intuition, or an uncanny ability to understand complex concepts with ease. Many feel deeply troubled by humanity's conflicts and environmental challenges, carrying a sense of responsibility to help shift these patterns.

What I've come to understand through years of channeling and spiritual exploration is that Earth is a crucial nexus point in the evolution of the Universe.

As creator beings in human form, we have the unique ability to work with matter in ways that energy beings cannot. We have fingers, hands, feet, mouths, and a variety of senses that allow us to do things that star beings and energy forms can not. This makes us essential partners in the Universe's ongoing evolution.

Each of us, whether starseed or otherwise, chose to be here at this precise moment in Earth's evolution. The specific circumstances of our birth - the time, place, family, and cultural context - were carefully selected to provide the exact conditions needed for our soul's growth and contribution.

I wish for you to come to your own conclusions about your soul's origin. Perhaps you don't align with the word starseed. Perhaps you might resonate deeper with angels, fairies, deities, or other spiritual forms. Please do not take my words as mere truth. It is important that you take the time to research, explore, and feel your way through these concepts and ideas. Wherever you feel that you come from, that is your truth, and I honor it.

My early exposure to both spiritual traditions and scientific exploration has created an ideal foundation and belief system for the work I do today.

My past has helped me develop a unique understanding of spiritual energy and consciousness from an ancient perspective, while paranormal documentaries have opened my mind to the vast possibilities beyond our planet. This unique combination has prepared me to understand and interpret information that I would channel from angels and energy or star beings beyond this realm.

Through all of my experiences, one truth has become increasingly clear: We are all far more than we appear to be.

Our physical forms are just the tip of the iceberg. We are spiritual beings who have chosen to experience life in this particular way, at this particular time.

And yet, the Universe within each of us holds infinite potential. Within you exists wisdom and truths that are inherently yours. You just need to awaken and remember how to connect with this wisdom and put it to good use. That is what your purpose is all about.

As we each recognize and embrace our spiritual origins, we can access more of our innate abilities and wisdom. This isn't about escaping humanity - it's about embracing everything about you while understanding your role in the greater cosmic classroom.

The challenges we face, the relationships we make, the lessons we learn - all are part of a grand design that we ourselves helped strategize before being born here on Earth. When we begin to understand and recognize this truth, we can live our lives with greater purpose and awareness, realizing that every experience, whether joyful or painful, serves the evolution of our soul.

"But how can I know what my purpose is?" many ask me.

"Listen to what has always called to you," I said. "The things that have fascinated you since childhood, the recurring themes in your life - these are the breadcrumbs leading you back toward your soul's original purpose."

For starseeds and curious souls, these breadcrumbs often include an early interest in day dreaming, abstract ideas, the Universe, or extraterrestrial life; recurring dreams of other worlds; a feeling of mission or purpose larger than personal goals; natural healing abilities; a deep compassion for humanity coupled with frustration about its limitations; and an intuitive understanding of energy, consciousness, and spiritual principles that seems to come from nowhere.

I want you to remember that your presence here is no accident. Whether you identify as a starseed, feel deeply connected to Earth's energy, or even if you don't believe in what I am saying, you are exactly where you need to be, having exactly the experiences you need to have. Your unique perspective, your particular challenges, your special gifts - all are essential parts of the Universe.

Each choice we make, every action we take, and every thought we think reverberates through the web of universal consciousness across multiple timelines, dimensions, and realities. We are literally shaping the evolution of the Universe through our earthly experiences.

Understanding or believing in a greater spiritual truth doesn't diminish the importance of our earthly lives - it enhances it. When we recognize ourselves as conscious participants in a greater evolution, every moment becomes an opportunity for growth, every challenge becomes a chance for transformation, and every relationship becomes a portal to greater understanding.

This is the profound truth that my father's scientific curiosity and my own spiritual experiences have both pointed to: we are spiritual beings having a human experience, creating and learning in ways that are unique to our current existence.

The way that I experience life will be vastly different from the way you experience yours. Where you were born, how you were raised, becomes 'data' for the Universe to understand what works or doesn't work. Why? Because the Universe is capable of creation, so are we.

As we gently open up to this understanding, we begin to access more of our innate truth, wisdom, and abilities, while becoming powerful and conscious channels for the light that we truly are. You are meant to be here on Earth. You are already here, reading this book. Within you, you are now creating possibilities, ideas, realities, and more.

Each of us has, within us, the wisdom of the stars and the creative power of the Universe to help us understand why we are here. Your purpose is not a mistake. Yes, you have a purpose - we all do.

You are not just a tiny fragment of a larger cosmic existence - you are a collaborator, partner, and participant in a Universal dance. We are both the audience and the actors in a theatrical play here on Earth.

This is the magic and wonder of our reality. As creator being, we can create or destroy anything with the power of our thoughts. Nothing is ever a mistake.

Chapter 3: Consciousness Unbound: The Quantum Perspective

Close your eyes for a moment and consider this: what if consciousness, the awareness of oneself and the perspective of the world, isn't limited to your brain, or even to your body?

What if this awareness is more like a field of energy that extends far beyond the boundaries of a physical form? This isn't just a random philosophical question - it's a path to understanding the true nature of your existence.

Let me share an experience that changed my understanding of universal consciousness forever.

During a particularly deep 'quantum meditation' - a meditation practice I've created and honed over years of spiritual exploration - I found myself floating up into the dark open landscape of the Universe. The word quantum here refers to an understanding and connection to the universe.

Before I continue with this story, let me take a moment to explain what meditation is and how quantum meditation differs from more traditional approaches.

At its core, meditation is the practice of training your attention and awareness to achieve mental clarity, emotional calm, and a deeper

connection to yourself. Traditional meditation comes in many forms.
- Mindfulness meditation, likely the most widely practiced form in the West today, involves paying attention to your breath, bodily sensations, or surroundings without judgment.
- Loving-kindness meditation focuses on developing compassion for yourself and others.
- Transcendental Meditation uses mantras (the repetition of words or phrases) to quiet the mind.
- Guided visualization uses imagery to promote relaxation and healing.

What all these traditional approaches share is their emphasis on calming the mind, staying present, and cultivating inner peace - these are all wonderful and valuable goals.

However, quantum meditation takes a different approach. Rather than looking inward or seeking stillness (which most people find difficult), quantum meditation encourages high levels of curiosity and imagination.

While traditional meditation often focuses on liberating the mind from streams of thoughts, quantum meditation specifically invites you to leverage your imagination to explore a realm of infinite possibilities that exists beyond our physical reality. It combines deep states of relaxation with focused intention to transcend ordinary consciousness and enter a state where the boundaries between observer and observed, self and Universe, begin to dissolve.

Think of it this way: if traditional meditation is like learning to be fully present in your house, quantum meditation is like discovering that your house has doors, windows, secret passages leading to the entire Universe - and then learning how to safely explore those realms while maintaining your connection to home.

In this practice, I use specific breathing patterns, visualization techniques, and frequency-based sounds to shift my brainwaves from beta (normal waking consciousness) through alpha and theta, and sometimes into delta and gamma states. These altered brainwave states allow consciousness to detach from its attachment to the physical body and expand into the quantum field, where time, space, and separation no longer apply in the same way they do in our everyday experience.

Rather than just observing thoughts as they pass by (as in mindfulness meditation) or repeating a mantra to transcend thought (as in Transcendental Meditation), quantum meditation involves actively directing your imaginative consciousness beyond physical limitations while maintaining complete awareness. It's like putting on VR goggles and completely immersing yourself in a new realm. It's more like an exploratory journey than a silent sitting practice, though it begins with many of the same foundations, including breath awareness and mental focus.

Back to my story...

With my eyes closed and in my inner vision, I looked downward, expecting to see hands and feet. I was struck by a confusing realization: in my quantum meditation, I had no form! I had no physical body, yet my awareness was more acute than ever.

In that formless state, something extraordinary happened.

My awareness exploded beyond anything I'd previously experienced. I understood that the Universe around me wasn't empty - it was alive and teeming with energy, wisdom, and truth, encoded in every particle of existence. I could feel the very molecules of energy pulsing with vibrant information, each one containing entire Universes of knowledge.

Consciousness, the understanding and connection to a Universe, isn't just a byproduct of our brain's chemistry. What allows us to be aware of our existence is a force of the Universe, as essential as gravity or light. When we limit our understanding of consciousness to neural brainwave activity, we are like fish trying to understand the concept of water by trying to study their own fins.

Think about those times when you've felt deeply connected to someone far away, or when you've known something without knowing how you knew it. What about a deja vu - how does that work?

These aren't anomalies or glitches in the matrix - they are glimpses of an already-existing expansive conscious awareness that is operating beyond the confines of your physical reality.

"How did you know I was thinking about you?" a friend once asked after I called her at the exact moment she was thinking of calling me.

"I just felt it," I replied, unable to explain why or how but certain of the intuitive connection. Is it possible that we are connected by invisible threads of energy? How curious.

Scientists have long puzzled over what they call "non-local consciousness" - the ability of consciousness to affect and be affected by events beyond the immediate vicinity of the brain. This becomes less mysterious when we understand that consciousness isn't actually produced by the brain, but rather flows through it, much like a radio receives rather than creates the music it plays.

Modern quantum physics has revealed that at the smallest scales, reality behaves in ways that are nothing like the solid, predictable world we experience with our senses. Particles can exist in multiple places simultaneously, influence each other instantaneously across vast distances, and even appear to alter their behavior based on whether they're being observed.

Quantum entanglement, one of the more fascinating phenomena in physics, happens when two or more particles become connected in such a way that the state of each particle cannot be described independently.

Let me explain this more clearly: Imagine two particles are created together in the same event, like two photons emitted from the same atom. These particles become "entangled" – fundamentally linked at their most basic level. Once entangled, these particles remain connected regardless of distance. If one particle is measured and shows a particular state (like spinning up), its entangled partner will instantly adopt a corresponding state (like spinning down), even if it's on the opposite side of the Universe.

Also, think of it like this: imagine two dancers who become so perfectly synchronized that when one makes a move, the other instantly makes a complementary move, no matter how far apart they are. There's no time delay, no signal passing between them – they are intuitively acting as one system, despite the physical space between them.

When particles are entangled in this way, they remain connected regardless of the distance between them. Change something about one particle, and its entangled partner responds instantly, faster than the speed of light. Einstein called this "spooky action at a distance" because it seemed to defy our conventional understanding of how the world works. This isn't just happening in laboratory experiments - it's happening everywhere, all the time.

Our bodies contain countless entangled particles of energy. Our thoughts and emotions create quantum energy fields that interact with the energy fields of others. When you suddenly think of someone and they call you moments later, or when you sense someone staring at you from across a room, you're experiencing quantum entanglement at a human scale.

Quantum meditation leverages these concepts and encourages our imaginations to run wild.

It was during one of these early quantum meditations that I first met Zee, my spirit team, a collective of hundreds of beings existing across different timelines, dimensions, and realities in the great Universe.

The beings (or aliens) appeared to me in various forms, sizes, and shapes, each bringing unique qualities, wisdom, and perspective. This might sound insane, but when we let go of our attachment to a specific type of physical form, we open ourselves to the true diversity of existence.

"Who are you?" I asked during our first meeting, sensing the enormity of their presence.

"We are a collective of beings," they responded, their voice echoing through my consciousness. "We exist beyond the boundaries of your physical perception, but we have always been connected to you."

I promptly named them Zee, due to the sheer number of beings. Zee is a nickname that speaks to all of them from A to Z. They taught me that consciousness isn't bound by the rules of physical reality. Just as quantum particles can exist in multiple states simultaneously, consciousness can operate across multiple dimensions and timelines. This is a practical truth that can transform your experience of reality today.

One of the most interesting aspects of quantum consciousness is its relationship to what psychologists call the shadow self—the aspects of ourselves that we have denied, repressed, or hidden from our conscious awareness.

The shadow self is a term introduced by psychologist Carl Jung to describe the parts of our personality that we've rejected or disowned. These might be traits, desires, or emotions that didn't fit with our family's expectations, society's norms, or our self-image. For example, if you were raised to believe that anger is always wrong, your natural capacity for the healthy expression of anger might have been pushed into your shadow.

Just as quantum physics demonstrates that particles exist in multiple states until they are observed, our consciousness contains multiple potential states of existence that remain hidden until we are ready to acknowledge them.

Shadows aren't inherently negative - they simply represent the aspects of ourselves we've learned to keep hidden in the dark. It might include our creativity if we were taught that art isn't practical, our anger if we learned that negative emotions aren't acceptable, or our power if we were conditioned to stay small and quiet.

Working with the shadow involves a process similar to quantum observation - by bringing conscious awareness to these hidden aspects, we change their state from potential to actual. This is why shadow work can feel so challenging yet transformative; we are literally changing the quantum state of our consciousness.

The process of quantum healing begins with acknowledging that these very shadows exist. Just as quantum particles can exist in multiple states simultaneously, we can hold space for seemingly contradictory aspects of ourselves. We can be both strong and vulnerable, both wise and learning, both human and divine.

"I'm afraid to tap into my anger because I might lose control," a client once confessed.

"What if your anger isn't just destructive?" I asked. "What if it also holds the key to your passion, your ability to set boundaries, thereby reinforcing your own power to create change? Are you telling me that you are going to let fear stop you because you're afraid of one emotion?"

When she realized this truth, she understood that the anger was the very key she needed to deepen the connection within herself and to create a new reality.

The ego - our sense of individual self - serves an important purpose in navigating this physical reality. Quantum consciousness, however, reveals that our true identity is far more fluid and expansive than the ego would have us believe.

Think of the ego as a unique wave pattern in the ocean of consciousness. It is real and serves a purpose, but it's not the total sum of what we are. The ego can only imagine and define what it can see and understand. The Universe, on the other hand, knows everything. Just as quantum particles can behave as both waves and particles, we can be both individual egos and infinite consciousness at the same time.

This understanding shifts how we approach personal growth and healing. Instead of fighting the ego or trying to transcend it, we can appreciate it as one of many possible states of our limitless consciousness and existence. It allows us to move fluidly between different states of awareness without becoming rigidly stuck to any of them. You are more than just your mind and body.

When we grasp the enormity of the quantum nature of consciousness, we understand that what we call "reality" is just one of infinite possible manifestations. Just as a quantum particle exists in multiple states until observed, our lives exist in multiple potential states until we collapse them into experiences through our consciousness.

In my own private quantum meditations, I've encountered and spoken with beings of pure light, geometric consciousness, shapes, blobs, colors, and forms of awareness that defy earthly description. Each encounter has taught me that consciousness is far more diverse and expansive than our human minds typically imagine.

Just as my spirit team Zee exists as a collective of hundreds of beings in various forms, consciousness itself can manifest in infinite ways.

"What possibilities would open for you," I often ask in workshops, "if you understood that you're not limited to a single timeline or a single version of yourself?"

The responses of ooooh's and aahhh's always reflect the quantum nature of our being - possibilities ranging from healing ancestral trauma to manifesting entirely new life paths.

Quantum meditation isn't about escaping our earthly reality but about expanding our awareness beyond it while remaining fully present in our human experience. It's about recognizing that we are infinite spiritual beings, capable of existing in multiple states and dimensions while maintaining our coherence as individual expressions of consciousness.

As you begin to explore consciousness beyond physical limitations, whether in my quantum meditations or not, you'll discover that everything - from thoughts to emotions to physical matter - is essentially energy in different forms of expression.

The boundaries between self and other, between physical and spiritual, begin to dissolve, revealing the underlying unity of all existence. That same level of awareness I experienced in the quantum realm is also available to you. It doesn't require special powers or decades of spiritual practice - it simply requires the willingness to open yourself to possibilities beyond your current understanding.

In the quantum realm, energy and consciousness are inseparable. Every thought you have creates ripples in the quantum field, affecting not just your immediate environment but the entire web of existence. When you have strong emotions, you are actually creating powerful waves of intentional quantum energy that can be felt by others, even across vast distances.

This understanding transforms how we view human interaction and relationships.

What we call "chemistry" between people is a resonance or similarity of the energy in the quantum fields. When you feel drawn to certain people or repulsed by others, you are sensing the measurement of the energy fields around them. If the energy between you and a person feels good, you are more similar in frequency. If the energy between you and a person feels tense and yucky, then you are different in frequency. Your ability to 'feel' energy happens at a level far deeper than physical appearance or personality - it happens in the realm where energy and consciousness merge.

The natural world also offers endless opportunities to experience the song and dance of energy and awareness. When you walk in a forest, you're not just moving through a collection of trees - you're immersing yourself in a network of conscious energy exchange. Trees communicate through quantum energy fields just as they do through their root systems. They respond to human emotions and consciousness, and if you quiet your mind enough, you can feel their response.

"Stand with your back against this old tree," I instructed a group during a forest meditation retreat. "Close your eyes and just notice what you feel. Allow your mind to relax and observe what arises."

"I feel like the tree is speaking to me without words," one participant shared. "I could feel its energy saying hello by moving through my body."

These feelings or thoughts are not just a part of your wild imagination - it is a direct experience of quantum consciousness, of energy communicating with other energies beyond physical means.

Even in urban environments, this frequency continues. Buildings can hold the energetic memories of all who have walked through them. City streets can vibrate with the collective energies of thousands of people existing in the same place. When you feel the 'vibe' of a particular place, you're sensing its quantum energy signature. Manhattan, New York, is a great example of this.

But wait, there is more. Your own body is a masterpiece of quantum choreography. Every cell in your body vibrates with intelligent energy, actively creating and transforming. When you are inspired, it's not just a mental phenomenon - it's a quantum event where higher frequencies of consciousness interact with your physical form. This is why creative insights often feel like they come from "somewhere else" - they literally do, arriving through quantum channels of consciousness.

When you look at a tree, try seeing it not just as a physical object, but as a particular configuration of quantum possibility made manifest through consciousness. When you interact with others, feel the quantum field that connects you beyond physical proximity. These practices aren't just figments of your imagination - they are practices that can expand your actual perception of reality.

The quantum song and dance extends deep to healing and transformation as well. When you direct loving thoughts and attention to a part of your body that's in pain, you're engaging in quantum healing, allowing higher frequencies of consciousness to interact with dense physical matter.

Here's how it works in practice: When you focus on sending good vibes to a specific area of discomfort, you're directing good energy to interact with the quantum field of that body part. This shifts the energy patterns at the subatomic level, which can then manifest as physical change or healing.

For example, in my energy healing sessions, I guide clients to first enter a deeply relaxed state through breath and visualization. Once they've shifted their brainwave patterns, I help them direct their awareness to the affected area while maintaining a state of open, loving acceptance. From this state, I will introduce healing frequencies – either through sound, visualization, or directed intention through my own quantum awareness – that resonate with the body's natural state of wholeness.

The fascinating part is that this process often creates measurable changes. I have seen clients experience reduced inflammation, accelerated tissue repair, and relief from chronic conditions and pain that haven't responded to conventional treatments. It also works on an emotional or mental level, increasing clarity, peace, connection to a higher power, and activating purpose. I've seen clients finally be free of nightmares, heaviness, or confusion. Despite this feeling like mystical wishful thinking, it's the practical application of quantum principles to biological systems.

This is the same principle that operates in all forms of energy healing, from ancient practices to modern modalities.

I've seen how consciousness can direct and shape energy at the quantum level. Intention becomes a force that can organize quantum fields into new patterns. This isn't metaphysical hocus pocus - it's the same principle that quantum physicists observe when they discover that the mere act of observation affects the behavior of particles.

You are not just a physical human being having occasional spiritual experiences - you are consciousness itself, temporarily expressing through physical form, here on Earth.

Your true nature is quantum, existing in multiple states and dimensions simultaneously. Every breath you take is an exchange of energy with the quantum field. This is why deep breathing helps you reset your mind and body. Every thought you think is a wave in the ocean of consciousness. Every act of kindness or creativity is you participating in the grand quantum dance of existence.

As you gently ponder this truth, you will naturally begin to embrace your role as a channel of light, capable of touching and transforming the very fabric of reality. Your existence as a channel of light is about recognizing what you already are - a magical, spiritual, quantum, energy being - dancing in the infinite field of consciousness, expressing the light of universal awareness and wisdom through your unique form of human experience.

You are indeed magic.

Chapter 4: Deprogramming the Subconscious: Breaking Karmic Patterns

When I was thirteen years old, my mother made a bold decision that would forever change the course of my life: she sent me to live and study at a Buddhist monastery halfway around the world, to be raised by monks and nuns.

This monastery, called the City of Ten Thousand Buddhas, has a vibrant Buddhist community, Dharma Realm University, and a K-12 boarding school nestled deep in Northern California.

Although her decision came from a place of answering a spiritual truth within her, it subsequently ripped my family apart, and ultimately, we would never be a family unit ever again.

While my classmates in Hong Kong roamed the hallways of our international primary school, I found myself walking the sacred (and strict) grounds under the mentorship of the Venerable Master Hsuan Hua, one of the most revered Buddhist teachers of our time in the West. This period of my life would ultimately lead me to understand the deep nature of karma, consciousness, and the patterns that shape our lives.

The City of Ten Thousand Buddhas was unlike anything I had ever experienced before.

Founded by the Venerable Dharma Master Hsuan Hua, it spanned 700 acres of pristine land, with a Buddha hall, study halls, and schools where people could find sacred refuge in the modern world. The Buddha hall is adorned with 10,000 hand-carved Buddha statues, which gives the monastery its name.

But what made the monastic experience extraordinary was the presence of Dharma Master Hsuan Hua himself, a true change maker whose teachings, wisdom, and compassion draw seekers from around the world.

Born in 1918 in northeastern China, Dharma Master Hsuan Hua had extreme spiritual sensitivity from a young age. At age eleven, after witnessing the death of a child in the wild, he contemplated the impermanence of life. He resolved to cultivate enlightenment and spirituality much like Gautama Siddhartha, the Buddha.

Following his mother's example of Buddhist devotion, he began bowing to the ground several hundred times daily as an act of compassion for all sentient beings.

Despite having a limited education in rural China, Dharma Master Hsuan Hua had extraordinary intelligence and a photographic memory. By sixteen, he was already teaching and lecturing on Buddhist sutras to villagers. By eighteen, he had mastered not only Buddhist texts but also Confucian classics, traditional Chinese medicine, astrology, divination, physiognomy, and the scriptures of the great religions. His commitment to service led him to establish a free school for impoverished children while still a young man himself.

At nineteen, he became a monk, and in 1959, he embarked on a mission to bring Chinese Buddhism to the West. He established the Dharma Realm Buddhist Association in the United States, fulfilling his vision to "create Buddhas and Bodhisattvas" in the Western world. Dharma Master Master Hua's teachings focused on direct mind-to-mind transmission of wisdom, rigorous ethical practice, and compassionate service to all beings - principles that would profoundly shape my life after I took my own formal vows with him as my Dharma Teacher. Though he passed away in 1995, his lineage continues through his disciples, including myself, who carry his spiritual teachings in the modern world today.

One afternoon, during my early days at the monastery, I heard that my parents' marriage was falling apart. I rushed to find Master Hua seated in the Buddha hall, speaking to each of his disciples one by one. Patiently, I waited in line for my turn to ask for clarity. It was an honor to speak with him directly, as he wasn't always available. My heart pounded with heaviness and worry as I asked him, "What can I do to help my parents? They are falling apart…"

His answer was not what I expected.

"It is not your business. Ignore them."

I walked away from that conversation feeling completely confused and devastated by his icy coldness. Was my Dharma Master having a bad day? He did not elaborate or leave me any clues. At thirteen, my little mind couldn't comprehend what he was trying to teach me. It would ultimately take years and decades before I truly understood the significant wisdom in his words: "It is not your business. Ignore them". I now understand that karma operates on multiple levels simultaneously, and that each soul must walk their path of learning. What he meant was that I could not possibly change my parents' karma - this was their lesson to learn, not mine. This understanding would later become an important part of my work helping others heal their wounds, patterns, karma, and relationship dynamics.

Dharma Master Hsuan Hua taught us that karma is like a web of connections, where each thread—personal, familial, and collective—interweaves with countless others. Our actions, thoughts, and behaviors ripple far beyond what we can see in our immediate experience, affecting not just our current life but also future incarnations.

Each person's journey is uniquely their own.

Now, in my present moments as an experienced spiritual mentor and practitioner, I apply the lessons I learned early in my client work. The wisdom that once confused me in my teenage years has become the foundation of my healing practice. This time, I can eloquently share wisdom with deep compassion and relevant context around the many life lessons.

I recently worked with a woman named Sarah who had spent

decades suffering from feelings of grief and abandonment. Despite being functional and successful, every romantic relationship she entered into always ended the same way - her partner would always leave her, leaving her with even more grief and abandonment. Flustered, she turned to me to help her understand and heal any spiritual, energetic, emotional, or mental blocks that were holding her back from finding true love.

During our session, I accessed her Akashic Records— a place in the quantum universe that stores information for every soul. I discovered that she had a past-life agreement created eons ago to help her learn and discover her own power.

All souls, including yours, carry karmic agreements or contracts to help us transform in our souls' evolution. These agreements may include relationships and experiences that can lead to joy, love, pain, and suffering.

The Akashic Records, where these contracts, agreements, life plans, lessons, and a plethora of other information are housed, can be understood as a universal database that contains every thought, action, emotion, and experience that has ever occurred in time and space. This database is non-physical and holds the complete history of every individual soul, including past lives, present circumstances, and future possibilities. When I access these records, I connect with a quantum field of information to retrieve insights about an individual's soul's unique journey, path, patterns, and life purpose. Imagine the possibilities if we can access what is hidden in the shadows of your soul to accelerate your healing and growth.

Through the Akashic Records, I discovered that Sarah's recurring abandonment was tied to one specific soul agreement around grief and abandonment. These contracts are not written like legal agreements or commitments, but are energetic. Agreements can be written before your birth, in soul form, to help shape your specific life path so that you can learn specific lessons. This is why many people refer to Earth as 'Earth School'. These agreements continue to exist in our energy field, despite many of us having no memory of them, and they have the power to influence our choices, relationships, and experiences at a subconscious level. Some agreements serve our highest good, while others may have outlived their purpose but continue to operate and renew automatically, creating recurring patterns of challenge or limitation without any way out.

Soul contracts are typically created and agreed upon during the soul planning process, between and before our human lives. In the planning meeting, we meet with our spiritual team, God, the Creator, or the Universe, and other ascended souls such as angels, archangels, or cosmic beings to plan for experiences that will push us into growth. We choose specific lessons, relationships, and challenges that will help us develop qualities like compassion, forgiveness, resilience, or inner strength. Sometimes, contracts are also forged during trying moments of transformation within a specific lifetime or era, when our soul makes a deep commitment to a particular path or lesson. I'm sure you know that not all contracts are pleasant. Many of us do not even remember our agreements. But they are designed to help our souls evolve for the greater good.

In Sarah's case, I could see the contract clearly in her energy field - it appeared to me, psychically, as a complex geometric pattern of light strands with several significant energetic distortions. The original agreement had become outdated, rigid, and inflexible. This contract had been established with other participating souls who would ultimately play the role of abandoning her, creating the specific chance for her to master the lesson of abandonment.

In a previous lifetime, Sarah was a spiritual teacher who chose to live her life in solitude as a means to enlightenment. She made a soul-level karmic agreement to experience separation from her community and loved ones as a way to develop raw spiritual strength. That contract had served its purpose in that particular lifetime, but it had continued to auto-renew through following human lives, creating a pattern of abandonment that no longer served her growth and made no sense.

Much like legal contracts with attorneys and lawyers, sometimes the fine print needs to be revised and updated for the change to take effect. For me to update a soul contract, I need to do a few things. First, I must psychically find and identify the original purpose of the agreement and understand if that lesson has been learned. Then, with clear intention and telepathic codes, I will use my shamanic gifts to speak to the highest spirit team(s) in charge and ask for permission to end or alter the agreement. Once permission is granted, I will do the energetic healing work to close the contract and create a new agreement that better serves the current path and purpose.

As I worked to update this contract with Sarah, I clairvoyantly witnessed the energetic ties beginning to dissolve, like stars blinking out one by one in the night sky. The distorted geometric pattern I had seen earlier shifted, releasing its patterns and reconfiguring itself into a more balanced and beautiful pattern. The relief that Sarah felt was immediate. When I opened my eyes, I could see that she had been crying while I was working on her energies. We both shared tears of joy as the energy flooded through our bodies, despite being behind our respective computer screens on Zoom. Within months, Sarah told me that she had been able to bring a different sense of connection to her friendships. Her heart was still tender in a romantic sense, but she was more trusting and ready for love's permanence.

Know this, our human patterns don't always stem from past lives. Sometimes they are created in our current lifetime, often in early childhood or in the womb. Another client, Michael, came to me struggling with persistent financial difficulties despite his successful career. During our session, I clairvoyantly looked at his chakras and into his Akashic records. I immediately connected with his six-year-old self, in this lifetime, who had witnessed his family lose everything in a financial crisis.

That experience caused so much chaos and instability that he made a subconscious decision that money is dangerous and can inevitably lead to suffering. This belief system created a pattern where Michael would unconsciously sabotage every financial opportunity.

Through chakra healing and inner child work, I was able to speak to that younger part of Michael and help him understand that he was no longer in danger. Much of my work involves conscious dialogue with the energetic, karmic, or psychic aspects of my clients' souls. In those conversations, I was able to release the energetic cords binding him to that early trauma. Michael's relationship with money evolved. Six months later, he reported not only financial growth but a newfound sense of peace and calm around money.

We all have aspects of ourselves that hold onto memories or patterns that may not serve us. During my time at the monastery, Dharma Master Hsuan Hua taught us about the nature of the shadow self - how those aspects can be consciously or subconsciously denied or hidden away.

"Even the darkest shadows," he would say, "are created by light. Without light, there would be no shadow at all."

This understanding made a lot of sense in my work with Maria, a gifted healer who struggled to accept her abilities.

During our session, I discovered a soul contract from a past life where she had been persecuted several hundreds years ago for her natural healing abilities. Whether this 'past-life' phenomenon is real or imagined, the past-life trauma created a deep fear around her intuition, causing her to dim and hide from her natural light in this lifetime, both consciously and unconsciously.

The contracted experience manifested in her energy field as a series of blocks that activated whenever she began to tap into her intuitive gifts more publicly. Those blocks showed up as energetic walls that would trigger high levels of anxiety, self-doubt, and even physical illness whenever she tried to grow her healing business. The contract essentially stated: "If I am seen using my spiritual gifts in a public way, I will be in danger."

As I worked to release this contract, I spoke to the persecuted version of Maria and told her that we live in a day and age where spirituality is no longer a secret practice. Confused, the persecuted Maria began to ask me a series of questions. She asked, "What era do you live in? What is your society like? Is spirituality condemned? Why is your world different now?"

I patiently answered each of them to help her understand the new timeline and reality in which we now live. I showed her a series of telepathic images of the changes of time throughout the centuries. Then, I guided the present-day Maria through a process of questions to merge and integrate new truths, allowing her to understand the original protective purpose of the agreement. In the end, I led her to choose a new contract - one that serves humankind consciously. The new soul agreement, for all versions of Maria, stated: "I am safe to shine my light brightly. My intuitive gifts are needed, and I am welcomed and necessary in the world."

I witnessed something powerful when this new contract took hold. Chills went down my spine as I telepathically understood a change had taken hold. The energetic web of past life traumas began to unravel, and with each thread that dissolved, Maria's natural aura grew stronger and brighter. The blocks that had once held her back transformed into an expansion of energy, allowing her gifts to flow freely, but with clear personal boundaries. She later shared with me that for the first time in her life, she felt safe fully expressing her gifts.

One of the most interesting things about working with karmic patterns and energies is understanding how energy healing can ripple and correct itself across multiple timelines. When we heal a pattern in the past, that healing extends both backwards and forwards, affecting past, present, parallel, and future timelines.

In another time, I experienced this ripple effect firsthand with a client named James, who also had deep ancestral trauma around persecution. As I worked to heal this pattern, I was shown by his spirit team how this healing would affect not only his own past lives but also the experiences of his descendants. The weight of generations of fear and hiding began to lift, creating space for new stories to emerge.

At the monastery, we learned that we can face our shadows through various practices, including intense periods of meditation and self-reflection.

Dharma Master Hsuan Hua would often say, "The things you run from, run you. The things you face, you can embrace."

Sometimes, we run from subconscious fears or experiences that we can not begin to understand. This is why my work is somewhat forensic. When working with my clients' shadow healing, I ensure that I am completely thorough in healing any timeline, reality, or dimension.

The process of deprogramming the subconscious and breaking karmic patterns in the Akashic records requires both (psychic) awareness and action. It begins with recognizing that many of our most challenging patterns aren't personal failures - they're often outdated programs running in the background of our spiritual operating system, like a computer.

Think of it this way: your soul has journeyed through many lifetimes, accumulating a series of experiences and forming patterns. Some of these patterns serve an important purpose in their respective time, but can limit your growth and personal expression today.

Just as you would update outdated software on your computer, your soul's programming sometimes needs to be updated to align with your current path and purpose.

I have learned, firsthand, about the power of the present moment in healing past wounds and vice versa. While past life regression and karmic healing can help us understand our patterns, actual healing always occurs in the present. This is where we have the power to choose differently, to rewrite new stories, to release what no longer serves us.

When I work with a client's inner child, we are not just visiting the past to look around - we are consciously integrating healing energy from the present moment into those old wounds. The adult self becomes a source of strength and wisdom for the younger self, or vice versa, creating a healing ripple that flows both ways through time.

I encourage you to pay attention to the areas of your life where you feel stuck, or where similar situations keep repeating themselves. These repetitive patterns can indicate deeper karmic patterns or subconscious programming that require attention.

If you've ever had emotional triggers that seem disproportionate to the triggering event, then it could mean that a past life wound has been activated.

If you find yourself in the same situations over and over again, despite consciously trying to make new choices, then that could also point to a karmic pattern or contract that needs updating.

Are there parts of yourself that you feel you have to hide or suppress? Those could be shadow parts of you waiting to be acknowledged, loved, and integrated.

Through my work with clients and my own healing journey

over the past twenty years, I have learned that true freedom comes not from trying to remove or ignore our patterns and shadows, but from leaning heavily and intentionally into them with loving understanding and compassion. Every pattern, wound, and hidden aspect of ourselves holds infinite wisdom and potential for expansiveness when properly understood and transformed.

The client whose karmic contract I helped update did not just experience a release; she gained access to the wisdom and strength she had learned through all those lifetimes of learning about power. The only difference was that she could now easily access those intuitive gifts without having to experience the associated trauma repeatedly.

Working with conscious, subconscious, and karmic patterns isn't about deleting our life history - it's more about freeing ourselves from unconscious and unnecessary programming that limits our present, parallel, and future. When we integrate light into our shadows, update outdated karmic agreements, and heal our inner wounds, we create space for new possibilities to emerge.

I learned that every limitation can be an illusion of the mind. When you recognize and release these limitations - whether they come from this lifetime, past lives, or ancestral patterns - you expand into more of who you truly are. This understanding has been reinforced countless times throughout my client sessions, as I witness their transformation after outdated patterns are finally released.

The deep work of deprogramming and healing all parts of us continues throughout our lives; it is never linear. Each level of awareness reveals new opportunities for growth and transformation. And with each step, we become conscious creators of our own reality, more capable of embodying our highest potential.

Looking back now, I understand that being sent to the monastery at the age of thirteen, though challenging at the time, was part of a larger pattern of spiritual preparation.

That experience gave me the foundation to understand the deep workings of karma, timelines, and consciousness, allowing me to help others navigate their own healing journeys.

What initially seemed like a painful separation from my family became an opportunity to learn the fundamental lessons of purpose.

I have come to see that every pattern, every challenge, and every seemingly difficult circumstance carries within it the seeds of transformation. When we approach our patterns with compassion, they become doorways to greater freedom and authenticity. The key is to remember that the past never limits us. We are always allowed to choose whatever feels right, to write a new story, and to allow more light into our shadows.

Chapter 5: The Hierarchy of Spiritual Guidance

    Back in Hong Kong, when I was around eight or nine years old, I would often hear ghostly footsteps in the middle of the night at our home in Happy Valley. Intuitively, I knew they were not human because each time I would call out to my parents, the footsteps would stop, and I could hear my parents snore through my pleas to calm my anxiety and fear. The footsteps would start at the farthest end of the hallway by the kitchen, and proceed closer and closer to my bedroom door at a steady pace. In Chinese culture, there are precise instructions about spirits or ghosts: never answer to your name if someone calls out your name after dark.

    Spirits that roam at night are not always kind, my family would warn. Some are looking for a physical body to replace their own that no longer exists. If you answer, you grant them permission to take your body, or worse, your soul.

    Though I was fascinated by these disembodied sounds, I would slowly pull the blankets over my head, squeezing my eyes shut while silently praying that the aliens would come and take me away. Yes, I was a bit of an odd child.

    My early experiences with the paranormal world planted seeds of curiosity that would flourish throughout my life. Each encounter led me to understand the concept of spiritual energies, remnant imprints, and earth-bound spirits. Yet, at the time, I had no framework to understand these experiences; I only had the cultural warnings that kept me safely tucked under my covers.

When I arrived at the City of Ten Thousand Buddhas, my sensitivities intensified in ways I could not have expected. What I've never shared in my background or history is that this monastery was built on the grounds of a former state asylum for the criminally insane - home to some of the most violent inmates ever to have been committed in California.

According to an article published by SF Gate in 2025, the property is home to approximately 1,600 people who have died at the asylum. It was home to the criminally insane and some of the most violent inmates ever to have been committed in California. This was information I was not privy to at the time.

The energetic imprints of these spirits remained deeply embedded in the land and buildings. While we, as children, had spiritual practices, the veil seemed awfully thin between dimensions, allowing energies to become more potent and powerful.

It wasn't uncommon for us children to see, hear, or occasionally sense things that most people would not see. One night, while walking to the bathroom, I could feel someone drifting behind me. As I walked faster, it followed closer. When I turned, expecting to see one of my friends, I was greeted by an empty space. This happened regularly, leading me to become unfazed and immune to phantom presences.

There are so many experiences like this that I can not even begin to describe what it was like to live amongst the dead, 24/7. Rather than fear, I felt a strange sense of curiosity, as though I was privileged to live in both our current reality and the invisible world.

These experiences at the monastery prepared me to work with the unseen, even though I didn't quite understand how psychic abilities worked at the time.

Dharma Master Hsuan Hua would occasionally address these paranormal experiences in his teachings, explaining that many different types of spirits exist throughout the various dharma realms. There are many planes of existence for spirits: earthbound, in between Heaven and Earth, Heaven itself, and Home. Some of these spirits may have achieved great wisdom and compassion, while others remained caught in cycles of suffering. Our human responsibility, he taught, was to maintain a high-vibration practice of prayer and meditation, which would naturally allow us to attract only positive influences and transform negative ones.

In my earlier adult years, as I began exploring spirituality beyond my traditional Buddhist upbringing, I started hearing the term "spirit guides." The concept both intrigued and confused me. Despite my sensitivity to invisible energies, I could not seem to connect the dots with these 'spirit guides' in the way many intuitives described. I would sit in meditation, clear my mind, and ask questions. But the answers would never come, and my time would feel forced and uncertain.

I felt out of tune with my spirituality, wondering if I had missed a step in my intuition. Or was I trying to conjure up the voices of spirit guides that truly do not exist? I found it so much easier to connect with the dead. But spirit guides were a whole other ball of wax.

As a Type-A personality with control issues, I needed to find a more structured approach to talking to my spirit guides rather than waiting for them to appear. My business background has trained me to seek clear frameworks and methods.

Everything changed quickly in the span of a few months when I met a group of spiritual friends on the app Clubhouse. In 2020, COVID transformed our lives, forcing us to stay at home.

The app allowed us to talk to people from around the world. My new friends – Bridget, Nimesh, Brittney, and Faye - would gather daily in our own private clubhouse, called "Awake and Ascending". Curious intuitives, spiritualists, and fans of the paranormal from all corners of the world would come to discuss spirituality and the meaning of life on earth. Hours and hours of deep conversations opened doors to an understanding about the Universe that my solo practice hadn't allowed me to access. As a club moderator, I openly shared my paranormal and spiritual experiences, allowing me to open up Pandora's box of cosmic and galactic mysteries. I became deeply fascinated with aliens all over again. Still, this time, I had a captive and engaged audience that would eventually lead me to develop my own meditation style: Quantum Meditation.

Quantum meditation is a type of visualization meditation that allows us to proactively travel through the Universe and explore any level of consciousness.

With this proactive approach, instead of waiting for my spirit guides to come to me, I would go directly to them, energetically and telepathically, to seek answers to my many questions about life, consciousness, the Universe, ghosts, aliens, and more. This took my psychic and spiritual gifts to a completely new level. People who meditated with me began to awaken and gained deep insights that were unattainable through traditional meditation.

During one particularly exciting quantum meditation, I found myself floating up into the Universe, into a space of pure light, where I saw an energy so vast and compassionate that tears began to flow from my eyes. The eerie emptiness spoke directly to my mind, not in words, but in complete concepts that unfolded within me like blossoming flowers.

Intuitively, I recognized one of the many presences in this space as Archangel Michael. Though I've seen photos of him in artist renditions, I could see every intricate detail of his outfit, sandals, wings, and sword. Yes, he had a full head of hair. And for some reason, I knew that he wasn't just a human with wings and a sword, but a multidimensional source of intelligence with intense compassion and power. He flashed his gear at me, as if to make sure I understood how powerful he is. Funny guy.

This experience was the first of many encounters with higher spiritual beings and guides, including Archangel Gabriel, Raphael, Mother Mary, Mary Magdalene, Jesus, and, of course, with the infinite presence that many traditions and religions call God – the creator of wisdom and truth that transcends all names and forms. Though I am religious, I find it easier to use these names to represent the energies because they are the most widely known. We can easily substitute the names of these beings for Buddha, Kwan Yin, Krishna, Ashtar, or anyone else that suits your personal belief system.

Meditation after meditation, I began to recognize the distinct levels of each spirit guide, much like corporate hierarchy, each serving a different role in our time of growth and awakening. I also deepened my friendship with each of them, talking to them as if I am talking to my best buds.

What I finally learned and understood is that connecting with spirit guides requires letting go of all expectations and allowing the place where your imagination lives to run wild. Yes, the place where your intuition exists is the same wavelength as where your imagination lives.

My own psychic abilities gradually opened through these experiences, emerging in different forms. Beyond my early clairsentience and claircognizance—the feeling of energies and knowing things—I began experiencing spontaneous clairvoyant visions, where I could see energy fields, spirit beings, deceased people, and scenes from other times and places on Earth with remarkable clarity. Sometimes these visions would appear in my mind's eye; other times, they would overlay my physical vision like a transparent film. I later developed clairaudience, hearing internal voices that would convey messages to me, or voices that came in like a radio channel being perfectly tuned. The most surprising part of my spiritual growth was my ability to channel - to set aside my ego and allow spirit guides to communicate directly through me, using my voice, to share information I had no way of consciously knowing.

These abilities, I later discovered, mirrored those of my Shang Dynasty shamanic ancestor, appearing in my life without any formal training, as if they were activated from my own DNA. Through curious practice, I learned how to deliberately use these psychic gifts whenever I wanted to, instead of having them appear randomly. This required me to develop the discernment to know who or what spirit guide or psychic channel was trying to come through at any given time.

As a spiritual seeker and mentor, I finally developed a robust framework of four distinct spirit levels, each serving a different purpose.

The first and highest level is the creator consciousness itself: God, Source, Creator, the Universe, or the Infinite Mind that designed and pervades all of existence. I see this level as the home of the CEO of the Universe; the ultimate intelligence from which all beings and dimensions emerge.

Connecting with this level of consciousness brings experiences of unity, boundless love, and the dissolution of all separation. Time and space as we understand them cease to exist, and we recognize ourselves as individualized expressions of this same infinite consciousness. When I am working with some of the darkest energies, I do not hesitate to call upon God himself.

The second level consists of the ascended masters and archangels – highly evolved beings who have either completed many cycles of physical incarnation (in the case of ascended masters) or were created as powerful administrators of universal energies (in the case of archangels). These beings operate primarily from non-physical dimensions but can project their consciousness into our realm when needed. They serve as teachers, protectors, and wayshowers for humanity's collective evolution.

Ascended masters include figures such as Buddha, Jesus, Kwan Yin, and Saint Germain, among many others who have transcended the cycle of rebirth through spiritual evolution and mastery. They are enlightened beings who may have once lived as humans. Each of them embodies and shares particular qualities of divine consciousness – compassion, forgiveness, transmutation, healing, and activation – and can be called upon for guidance in developing these qualities within ourselves.

Archangels, on the other hand, are powerful angelic beings that have never existed in physical form, but they serve as divine overseers and administrators of divine energy in the Universe, with specific roles.

Archangel Michael brings protection and truth, cutting away what no longer serves our highest good. Archangel Gabriel works with communication and acceptance, helping us express our truth and receive divine messages. Archangel Raphael brings healing on all levels – physical, emotional, mental, and spiritual.

You don't have to believe in them to feel their existence; they operate beyond the limitations of human faith systems, through our thoughts, prayers, and intentions, which allow them to merge into our reality to guide and support.

The third level includes our personal spirit guides, fairies, earth elements, angels, cherubim, and ancestors – spiritual beings who have a more direct connection to our individual soul journey here on Earth. Spirit guides can be souls we've known in past lives who now help us from beyond the veil. Some of them may be with us for our entire lifetime, while others come for specific periods or purposes. Ancestors are family members who have passed on but maintain a loving connection with their descendants, offering protection and guidance. Suffice to say, you don't need to know them personally for them to watch over you protectively.

I've found that many people who struggle to connect with their spirit guides or ancestors are being too formulaic and calculating about who they're willing to receive help from or when they demand them to appear. Don't wait for a dramatic encounter with an archangel where their wings fill your room, or for your Great-Grandmother Emma, who passed thirty years ago, to walk through the door. Spiritual connection is always subtle.

The fourth level – which is where many begin their exploration of the unseen – consists of remnant energies, personal energy fields (auras), earthbound spirits, demons, or imprints. This category is closest to our physical existence and, therefore, often easiest to feel and see, but it also holds the most confusion and potential for misinterpretation.

The phantom footsteps I heard as a little girl likely belonged to this level – perhaps an old soul who had lived in our home before us, replaying its life in a loop like a movie or song stuck on repeat. The energies I felt at the monastery were also likely in this same category - people and energies left in the environment by those who had had good, bad, or ugly experiences and refused to leave.

While I don't discourage people from exploring the paranormal, hauntings, and earthbound spirits, I always caution my students to approach them with the highest level of spiritual protection, discernment, and preferably, direct guidance from higher spiritual sources in the first, second, or third levels. Many of these lower-vibration entities and energies are neutral, but some spirits can be confused souls who haven't fully transitioned and learned how to drain or influence sensitive people negatively. I have performed enough entity removals and exorcisms to know that not all spirits are made equal; not all are nice and sweet. Some of them can and will deliberately leech off your human energies in order to fuel their ghostly existence. This is why traditional cultures have so many protective practices around spirit communication and connection.

When I am working with clients who are just awakening to their spiritual gifts, I always emphasize the importance of starting their practice by connecting with the highest spiritual sources first – establishing a relationship with Source/God/Creator and then working with ascended masters and archangels, before exploring connections with personal spirit guides and ancestors. This creates a foundation of protection and clear discernment, making the exploration of the immediate energetic environment much safer. If I were to make a comparison to the corporate world, you'd want to work with the highest-level executive or CEO available, right?

Developing your intuitive gifts – whether clairaudience (clear hearing), clairsentience (clear feeling), clairvoyance (clear seeing), claircognizance (clear knowing) or any other 'clair' – becomes more straightforward when you understand this framework. Each person will naturally gravitate toward one or two primary intuitive gifts, though all of them can be developed with practice. Note: You can't choose what your specific gifts are; you must allow your intuition to guide them. I find that many people demand to have clairvoyance, only to realize that they have had clairsentience all along but have chosen to ignore it.

Clairaudience, which literally means 'clear hearing,' is the ability to receive intuitive information through sounds, words, or thoughts that aren't physically audible but are heard through one's inner hearing.

Those with natural clairaudience might first notice the inner sounds as their own thoughts, but somehow feel different or the same as their own mental voice. Some may hear actual sounds.

One of my students recently recalled suddenly hearing an inner voice yell "Stop!" right before a car ran a red light where she was about to step into the crosswalk. Though it sounded just like her own mental voice, this inner guidance likely came from a spirit guide, angel, or ancestor watching over her journey.

Clairsentience, or 'clear feeling,' allows one to receive intuitive information through physical and emotional sensations - feeling the energy, emotions, or physical conditions of people, places, or situations. People with clairsentience can receive information through their own physical and emotional sensations, which can be difficult to distinguish from their own physical and emotional feelings. They might experience goosebumps when something is true, stomach tightness when something is off, or sudden emotional shifts when entering different environments. They might brush it off as a figment of their imagination, not realizing that they are picking up psychic information. My own clairsentience developed during my years at the monastery, where I could often feel the emotional states of other people. Because I didn't know how to differentiate between my own feelings and those of my friends, I thought everyone was mad at or hated me, not realizing that everyone has their own insecurities.

Claircognizance, meaning 'clear knowing,' manifests as receiving complete packets of information (like downloads) without knowing how you know - it's direct knowledge that arrives fully formed in your mind without a clear source. Those with claircognizance simply 'know' things without logical explanation – information drops into their awareness as complete packages of understanding. This often happens when connecting with the highest levels of guidance, where communication happens beyond verbal language. During my quantum meditations, when I am connecting with Source consciousness, I will frequently receive complex spiritual concepts as instant downloads of understanding that would take pages to explain in words.

Clairvoyance, or 'clear seeing,' is the ability to receive visual information beyond normal sight - seeing energy fields, spirits, symbols, images, movies, or scenes either with the physical eyes or, more commonly, within the mind's eye. Many people assume this is the most common psychic ability, but it tends to develop later for some simply because it is so subtle. Again, many brush off these psychic visions as a figment of their own imagination.

I remember one specific moment of clairvoyance during a group meditation when I clearly saw golden light pouring into a friend's chest area – the next day, she shared that she'd been diagnosed with a heart condition and was beginning treatment. She had prayed for divine healing, and it was being delivered.

Whatever intuitive gifts come the most naturally to you, know that you can strengthen them with regular practice and knowing who, what, or where you are connecting to in the Universe. Every guide, dimension, timeline, or reality has its own 'frequency' or vibrational signature. Every spiritual being communicates in their own unique way.

The way Jesus communicates with me is very different from how God appears in my meditations. The way that Archangel Michael flashes into my mind's eye is very different from how Archangel Gabriel will slowly emerge into my aura.

One simple, yet powerful practice for developing stronger spiritual connections is what I call an "energetic expansion meditation." Start by grounding your energy into the Earth. Then, intentionally reach upward from the base of your spine in your root chakra, connecting to each one until you reach above your crown chakra. Finally, rise into Creator consciousness. Sit in this energetic connection and use your imagination to bring the energy all the way back down from above your head, reaching through the soles of your feet and into the Earth below once again. Once you've established a column of energy or light through your body, you may begin to expand the energy wide beyond the confines of your physical body. Allow the energy to reach out by a few feet, noticing or imagining what comes up. Continue to do this until you feel a shift in your energy. Many of my students report feeling expanded, light, or experiencing profound inner peace.

From this place of energetic connection, you can invite any of your angels, ascended masters, or preferred archangels most aligned with your current needs or journey. Please invite any spiritual beings that feel comfortable to you and your spiritual belief system. Only after establishing a connection with these high-frequency beings should you then reach out to personal spirit guides, ancestors, or become receptive to the energies in your environment.

This approach ensures that your intuitive channels open in a sacred, protected space, filtered through higher frequencies first. This can be compared to installing a good water filtration system at home. Before you turn on the faucet, you'll get clearer, purer water or information this way. I caution this to protect you from opening your energies to just anyone or anything. Always ask to only work with those in the highest frequency.

For my clients who are constantly overwhelmed by nearby energies and earthbound spirits, I always start by helping them strengthen their connection to themselves. Planting your awareness deep in your physical body allows you to become grounded and not floaty. From there, we connect to Source consciousness, ascended masters, archangels, and so on and so forth. This creates a kind of energetic immunity and self-awareness, where your intuition becomes so connected to your body that higher frequencies can inspire you more than lower ones, which can drain you.

A client once beautifully described this practice as "tuning your radio to heaven's frequency". When you are so grounded in your own body before receiving the heavenly music from above, the static from below becomes background noise rather than overwhelming interference. This doesn't mean that you are becoming insensitive to earthly energies, but rather developing the discernment to engage with energies more intentionally.

The most important thing to remember about spiritual guidance is that authentic higher guidance always honors your free will and inner wisdom. Any spiritual message that creates fear, demands compliance, or makes you feel smaller rather than more empowered is absolutely suspect, regardless of how it presents itself. A loud, big, or resounding intuitive voice or sensation does not always make it a higher frequency. Trust what you are feeling.

True guidance from the higher levels of spiritual hierarchy feels expansive, loving, and aligned with your deepest truth, not fears, even if it challenges you to grow beyond current limitations.

My years of exploring these realms, from those first frightening footsteps in Hong Kong to universal connections through quantum meditation, have shown me that we are never truly alone on our spiritual journey. We exist within a vast and compassionate Universe populated by limitless beings at different stages of our evolution, many of whom are committed to supporting our growth and awakening.

Remember that the goal of your spiritual journey isn't to have dependence on outside entities, but rather to have an expanded awareness of our interconnection with all levels of consciousness. The hierarchy I've described isn't about bragging that some beings are more important than others – it's about understanding the different functions and frequencies of consciousness throughout the Universe so that we can navigate our truths with the purest wisdom and discernment. If you entered a retail clothing store and had an issue that needs to be resolved, would you spend your time arguing with a store clerk or would you escalate the issue and ask for the store or district manager?

The most powerful and meaningful intuitive guidance ultimately comes from within us – from the spark of light that exists in each of us, connecting us directly to Source. You must first learn how to trust yourself. Outside influences, guides —whether archangels, ascended masters, or loving ancestors —can help us clear the pathways to our own inner knowing. But you must be willing to trust.

Your team will always reflect to you aspects of your divine nature that you might not yet fully recognize or embody.

In time, you'll find yourself becoming a clearer channel for an infinite truth and for powerful healing energies to flow through from you, then to others. This is how we become conscious participants in a greater spiritual hierarchy – not just receiving guidance for the sake of being obedient, but embodying and transmitting any of our light in our unique way. This is what it truly means to be a channel of light in service to the evolution of a higher consciousness here on Earth.

Chapter 6: Awakening Intuition and Channeling Mastery

The very first time I channeled spiritual and divine information from realms up above, I was both electrified and terrified. In my early 40s, I had been meditating on a daily basis for months as a commitment to deepening my intuition after a serious bout of depression. I had hit rock bottom at that time and had no choice but to trust a higher power. Over time, I noticed the changes in my awareness - insights that would flow into my mind seemingly from nowhere. I could tell the difference between the abrupt incoming information and their frequencies, allowing me to clearly identify who was speaking to me.

But this one experience was different.

It was just an average day when I slipped into my quantum meditation. I felt my inner awareness expand beyond my body, connecting to a power that seemed greater than this Earthly realm. Almost like unlocking an invisible encyclopedia, I came to understand wisdom and truths that exceeded my own thoughts.

My throat tightened, but not in an anaphylactic way. Rather, an invisible energy was trying to open up my throat chakra to 'speak'. I took a few more deep breaths, clearing my mind and allowing emptiness to take its place. Words formed in my mind that gradually spilled from my lips without conscious thought. Before continuing, I hit record on my phone to capture the transmission. When I later listened to it, I could barely recognize my own voice, both in its tone and accent.

Many people believe that channeling and psychic gifts are rare. They assume these abilities are limited to a few chosen individuals. The truth is that anyone can tune into a higher power and access the information if you are willing and ready. It is your spiritual birthright, just waiting to be awakened and refined. Similar to strengthening specific muscles in our body at the gym, our intuition and psychic gifts can be enhanced with regular practice and proper technique.

Your intuition is not something separate from you; it exists as the voice of a higher power within your soul. Imagine having a radio receiver that is part of your DNA in your soul. That radio receiver can tune into frequencies beyond your natural five senses, as a sixth sense - it already belongs to you, you just have to turn it on. Some individuals can pick up frequencies more easily, but developing this skill just takes practice. The intuitive messages will come to you in different ways; there is no one-size-fits-all.

Remember our earlier discussions of clairsentience, claircognizance, clairaudience, and clairvoyance in the previous chapter? These represent some of the main ways through which intuition can flow through you. Most people have one or two primary 'clairs', although there is no hard rule.

To awaken your intuition, start by identifying your natural strengths. This doesn't mean strengths like being the best tennis player, writer, or dancer, but rather the qualities that make you who you are. What were you like as a child? Quiet, introverted, inquisitive, curious, or bossy? I was always bossy, if you couldn't guess by now.

Consider how you processed information when you were younger. If you were extra sensitive, like I was, perhaps you would experience it through clairsentience (clear feeling) - naturally picking up on others' emotions and energy. If you were extroverted and loved talking to people, perhaps you experienced it through clairaudience (clear hearing) - catching insights through inner sounds or words. Those who were visual learners might lean toward clairvoyance (clear seeing), experiencing intuition through mental images or visions. And if you were the child who just "knew" things without being able to explain how, you may have natural claircognizance (clear knowing) - receiving direct downloads of information.

Think back to a time when you received a piece of information that seemed to come from beyond your five senses, and it later proved to be accurate. Maybe like a dream, deja vu, body chills, or a random download - did you see an image, hear words, feel a sensation in your body, or just know it without logical explanation? These experiences offer clues to your primary 'clair'.

I see this a lot, but many tend to gaslight themselves into thinking that our intuition is fake or not good enough. Please understand that your intuition is designed to be extra subtle, because if it were accessible like everyday noise, you'd never pay attention.

One of the most effective practices that I have used in my own journey to awakening is what I call an 'intuitive check-in'. Every morning, before your morning coffee, ask the Universe for guidance or direction on what you need to focus on today or do. Do this while your mind is still in that receptive state between sleep and being fully alert. You can ask specific questions ("Should I accept this job offer?") or general ("What do I need to know about my day right now?").

Next, without thinking too hard, write down whatever comes to your mind. Don't overthink it - just write. Journal any images, feelings, words, or concepts. Don't judge or analyze what you're writing; just let it flow. Later in the day or week, read what you wrote and compare it to how your day went. Did you follow the intuitive guidance, or did you dismiss it because it felt cheesy?

The practice of writing down what comes to you before your intellectual mind jumps in allows you to strengthen your trust in these intuitive check-ins. If you revisit your notes at a later time, you might notice how accurate they were, even if you don't think so. Intuition does not flow from a place of judgement; it comes from a place of total self-trust.

Another powerful daily practice involves slow, mindful pauses throughout your day. Set an alarm to remind you three to five times a day to stop whatever you are doing and become fully present with your emotional, physical, mental, and spiritual status. Being present means being fully immersed in your five senses and noticing, soaking in every aspect of what you are feeling in your environment. Not in the past or the future, but right here, right now.

Start by taking three slow, deep breaths and feeling the energy in your heart space. Then, silently ask, "What do I need right now?" Notice what comes up, even if it feels fake or imaginary. It might be a subtle feeling, an image or moving picture, a knowing, or just a shift in your energy. These little moments of self-reconnection will help you become more in tune with your intuition.

A client of mine, Sophia, practiced these intuitive exercises faithfully for just two weeks. On the fifteenth day, she paused to feel into her heart chakra, just before she was about to sign a legal document. In that moment, she felt a distinct heaviness in her body and heard the words "Not yet" in her mind. With this information and the desire to trust herself more, she decided to wait and review the contract again. The next day, she discovered a clause in the contract that would have severely limited the rights to her own creative work. Had she not paused to check in with her intuition, she would have signed away her intellectual property and been stuck with that agreement.

As your intuitive awareness strengthens, you can explore more advanced techniques to channel information with your spirit team. Channeling differs from general intuition in its depth and source. While intuition often represents a communication with your higher self or spirit guides, channeling typically involves temporarily stepping aside to allow your consciousness to take a backseat, so that a higher frequency, energy, or collective consciousness can communicate with you more clearly and directly.

There are many forms of channeling, ranging from automatic writing or vocal channeling (where you remain fully conscious but receive downloaded information) to full trance channeling (where your awakened consciousness completely steps aside). For most people, I recommend starting with automatic writing because it allows you to see and feel what is happening in your body beyond your ordinary thinking mind.

A powerful method to start automatic writing is what I call the "Golden Light Meditation." Begin by getting into a comfortable seated position, making sure you won't be disturbed for at least 20 minutes. Ground your energies by imagining roots reaching down from your bottom into the Earth, and bringing the energy back up into your body to the top of your head to stabilize the energy. Then, imagine a protective, shimmery, sparkly glowing light around your body - this creates a high-frequency container for divine energies to flow through you.

Following this, set a clear intention for the type of information or wisdom you wish to channel. Be specific with this process. Silently say to spirit guides, "I want to connect with the highest frequencies and open myself to channel wisdom about my spiritual path," or "I invite my highest spirit team to connect with me for the highest good of all concerned. Please show me what I need to know." This specificity creates a focused invitation and helps prevent unwanted energetic influences.

Once you have connected to the energies, whether it is real or imagined, have your pen and paper handy so that you can start to write down anything that comes to mind. If computer typing is more your style, then make sure your fingertips are on the keyboard so that you can allow the words to flow through you, bypassing your desire to control anything. The key here is not to stop your writing, allowing a free flow of consciousness to run through you.

As you continue with this practice, imagine your consciousness expanding upward in a spiraling motion, connecting with the source you've invited to communicate with you. When you feel a shift in your energy, even if it is super tiny - perhaps a tingling sensation, a change in your breathing, or a feeling of expansion - begin to write down the words without pausing to fix any typos. Just write. Allow the words, images, or ideas to flow through you without judgment or analysis. If you find yourself overanalyzing the words being written, take a deep breath in through your nose and audibly exhale to reset your energy. Just acknowledge the thoughts and say, "Thank you for letting me know. I'm busy right now." Then, start over again with calling in your spirit team.

When I teach this method in workshops, I often hear people say that they are worried about "making it up" or "imagining things." Yes, you might be. But what does it matter? Intuition exists in the place where our imagination runs wild. Your skepticism is natural - our logical minds want to categorize and explain these experiences, especially new and unfamiliar ones. I remind my students and clients that imagination and intuition use the same neural pathways in the brain. You will feel like you are daydreaming and conjuring up images. Yes - trust that feeling and write anything down. The difference is not in how the information comes in, but in allowing yourself to trust yourself. The quality, consistency, and evidential validation of your automatic writing will improve over time and with experience.

Authentic channeled wisdom typically holds wisdom and truth beyond your current knowledge set and presents the information in ways you wouldn't normally express it. It might feel like it is coming from left field - trust that. There is no right or wrong way to receive information. The same goes for the information itself - there is no right or wrong information. Just make sure to feel into your body and use the entire body to assess whether it is you or not. If it feels heady, then you will want to reset by taking a big breath in and, when you exhale, feel into your entire being.

A student of mine, James, was convinced he was 'just making up' the information during the Golden Light Meditation until he channeled information about how to heal a family relationship. In our session together, I guided him to the frequency where information about his family existed. Then, I prompted him with questions that would allow his intuition to go deeper. What he received included facts and feelings from people that he couldn't possibly have known consciously. When he trusted the information and later spoke with his relative, he learned that the information he channeled was actually accurate, down to specific issues that had occurred years prior.

It's important to note that if you play the comparison game (ie, her psychic gifts are better than mine or I'm not good enough yet), those thoughts can lead to the beginning of the end of your intuition. Intuition requires trust. If you add doubt or projected fear into your energy field, you will definitely lose it. Those who are inspired to deepen their channeling abilities know that consistent practice will bring them results and help them discover more of their 'clair' gifts. When I work with clients, it typically takes about 5-10 minutes for us to practice together and establish that they are indeed channeling, simply because I can tune into the energies they are downloading and validate them on the spot.

Voice channeling - speaking aloud the information that comes through your voice - can be extremely powerful and difficult. This practice starts once again with the Golden Light Meditation, but includes specific attention to your crown and throat chakra, the energy centers associated with communication.

As you prepare to channel vocally, imagine your crown chakra, located at the top of your head, opening like a lotus flower, creating a clear path for information to flow down into your throat chakra.

Gently soften your body, relaxing the muscles, and allow divine energy to flow through you. Some people will resist words flowing through their voice because it feels uncomfortable (this is sometimes the case for me). Just be mindful of what you're experiencing and notice if you're in resistance. When I am channeling, I will relax my entire body but still use my intellectual mind, which has stepped aside, to translate the energy that comes to me. It might be a feeling, an awareness, a sensation, a pressure, or more. Do not compare how I feel it to how you might feel it. Be open.

Try saying simple phrases like "I am open to divine wisdom flowing through me now" or "I speak truth with love and clarity." Notice how your voice feels - its resonance, tone, and the sensation of sound moving through your body. Be patient with yourself. Allow your speaking to become more spontaneous, just let whatever words or phrases flow without planning or overthinking what comes next. Record these sessions if you can, as the information often contains insights you may not fully understand at that precise moment.

During channeling, I like to have a series of questions prepared so that I can ask the higher powers for answers. Perhaps it sounds like a conversation with yourself, but when you ask a question to your higher self, an ascended master, or a spirit guide, just trust what comes through. Channeling can be tricky if you don't know what to ask, but with the right amount of trust and patience, you can start downloading information leading you to a new level of awakening.

Personally, I enjoy having conversations with my spirit team, asking questions as if I'm talking to my best friend on the phone. This interactive approach often yields great results because no matter what, the information will only make sense to you. Just remember not to gaslight yourself. The way that I talk to my spirit guides is quite personal. Since I have been working with them for a long time, I have a personal relationship with them, just like with my best buds. I will often start with, "Hey, how's it going? What should I be focusing on today? What's the big picture here? Okay.... what else do I need to know?" I trust and allow all of the information, whether it is real or imagined, to flow through me. I treat every conversation with the utmost respect and do not doubt what is coming through.

If channeling sounds interesting to you, you might want to start testing out different types of spiritual communication beyond the basic channeling methods I've shared. There is no one-size-fits-all approach, except to allow anything and everything to flow through you. Also, the rules of communication are no shame, no guilt, and no judgment.

Telepathy - direct mind-to-mind communication - often happens spontaneously during channeling practice. It will also feel like it exists in the same place where your imagination lives. You might receive complete thought forms or concepts that open up in your awareness without being translated into specific words or images first.

This type of communication is actually more common with higher-dimensional beings, who typically don't think in human spoken words but rather in holographic concepts that contain multiple layers of meaning. For beginners, you may receive colors, feelings, and sensations. You'll want to play with this way of communication, allowing yourself to have fun and not take yourself too seriously.

Empathic channeling involves temporarily feeling into the emotions or physical sensations of another person or consciousness with which you want to connect. This form of channeling can be powerful for those who want to go deeper into medical intuition. Still, it requires stronger energetic boundaries to prevent oneself from becoming overwhelmed by the other person's energy. If you try this way of connecting, you will want to clear your energy field immediately afterward and disconnect. You can use a visualization meditation, sound healing, or physical movement to release any leftover energies that aren't your own. I prefer clapping because it's both a sound and a movement - I will usually clap until I feel the connection is gone.

Symbolic communication often occurs through the appearance of recurring symbols, numbers, or patterns that carry specific meaning. Most people recognize 11:11, 222, 333, 444 (also known as angel numbers), or any other sequence of numbers. Many people learn to trust these signs over time. Pay close attention to recurring symbols or numbers in your daily routine, keeping a journal of what you are sensing or receiving. Personally, I do not overthink angel numbers. Instead, I simplify the experience and see it as a reminder that I am on the right path. If you overthink the angel numbers, you might miss the others that are meant for you. I remember a time when I started seeing 11:11 over and over again. Another time, at the gas station, my fuel charges came out to $78.90. I took this as a personal sign that good things were finally on their way - a confirmation. I can't tell you what these good things are because it's private, but yes, good things have indeed arrived in my life!

For those interested in developing their clairvoyant abilities - seeing psychic information visually - regular practice with visualization and imagination (or daydreaming) strengthens the brain's neural pathways involved in this form of intuition.

Visualize a simple object, such as a lemon, with your eyes closed. It doesn't have to be a lemon; it can be an apple, a flower, a geometric shape - holding each object as clearly as possible for several minutes. You'll want to add more dimension to this experience, not just seeing, but imagining that you are feeling, smelling, hearing, or tasting the object. As this becomes easier with practice, move to visualizing more complex scenes or movies, allowing spontaneous images to appear in your mind's eye without consciously creating them. Clairvoyance is not always as it is depicted in movies - it's not seen using your physical eyes, although this is true for some people. It's more like a fleeting sensation in your inner mind that feels like you're imagining things or daydreaming. This is why I keep saying that telepathy, intuition, clair gifts, or channeling feel like they exist where your imagination exists. Trust the process and keep leaning into it. Do not gaslight yourself, please!

Working with a partner who holds an object in a sealed envelope or an oracle card provides another exercise for developing clairvoyance. This can definitely be more challenging, but well worth the experience. Without knowing what the other person is holding in their hands, close your eyes and feel into the energy of the object in their hands. Ask your spirit guides to receive visual information about the object. Open your mind and allow anything to flow through. You'll want to share out loud whatever comes to mind, whether it makes logical sense or not. Try to add dimensions and depth to what you sense, see, or feel. Are there colors, shapes, people, places, or something else? When the other person finally shares what they are holding, make a note of any correlations between your first impressions and the actual object. With practice, your accuracy will improve, and you'll learn to feel more accurately into the energy of the object and distinguish between imagination and true clairvoyant perception.

With all of these practices, remember to maintain a strong energetic boundary and grounding practice. Disconnect any leftover energy from you, even if it is spiritual. Lastly, being too esoteric, magical, and feeling 'out there', can leave you feeling even more disconnected in your real life. Before and after any channeling or intuitive development work, always take time to:
- Create a sacred space through prayer, intention setting, or rituals that feel meaningful to you.
- Ground your energy by connecting with the earth's stabilizing force, either through visualization or physical practices like walking

barefoot on natural ground.
- Set clear boundaries for the type of energies and information you're wanting to receive, specifying that all information must be for your highest good and the good of all concerned.
- Activate energetic protection through visualization of protective light, calling in your spiritual teams, or other protective practices from your spiritual tradition.

One of the most common problems people encounter when developing channeling abilities is the pesky interference of their analytical mind. Our everyday thinking tends to question, doubt, and attempt to control the natural flow of intuitive information. Remember that this is perfectly natural - your analytical mind is simply doing its job of keeping you safe and making sense of your experiences.

Instead of fighting yourself, invite your thoughts to become a cooperative partner in your spiritual and channeling practices. Ask your thoughts if there is something it needs to tell you. What does it want you to know? If it is not urgent, then gently set it aside and return to emptying your mind. I find that having a stern talk with my intellectual mind helps, even if it feels weird talking to myself.

I teach my students and clients to mentally assign their analytical mind a productive role during channeling sessions. You might imagine your analytical mind as a helpful assistant sitting close by, ready to take notes on the wisdom flowing through but not interrupting the process. You can also ask your analytical mind to serve as a gentle filter, helping you translate higher-dimensional concepts into human language without distorting their essence.

These approaches acknowledge the value of your analytical mind while preventing it from blocking the channeling process.

An effective exercise for navigating this balance in your mind is what I call "Channeling Conversations." In this practice, you deliberately switch back and forth between channeling and analytical reflection. Begin by channeling for 5 to 10 minutes, recording your session, whether it's written, spoken, or in another form. Then, consciously shift to your analytical mind and review what came through, noting any questions or insights. Next, go back to your channeling state, bringing these questions with you. This creates a collaborative relationship between your intuitive and analytical thoughts rather than setting them against each other. You are ultimately a team, but both of you can not be operating at the same time.

You might notice distinct qualities associated with different sources of channeled wisdom. The energy and information from your higher self typically feels intimately familiar yet elevated beyond your normal awareness. Communication from angelic presences often carries a frequency of profound love and light that may bring tears or a sense of expansion in your heart center. God's energy, or the Universe, feels vast and powerful. Ascended masters each have their distinctive energetic signatures - Christ consciousness typically conveys unconditional love and gentle strength, while Buddha nature often brings a quality of peaceful clarity and compassionate detachment.

Learning to distinguish these different energetic signatures helps you understand the source of the wisdom flowing through and allows you to intentionally connect with specific guides or teachers according to your specific needs. Because I have been channeling for a long time, I'm able to tune specifically into a frequency to call in a specific being. It's the same idea of memorizing phone numbers and knowing which ones to call or text when you need to speak to someone specific.

With practice, you'll develop what I call "spiritual recognition" - the ability to recognize not just who you're channeling, but also the level of truth and relevance in the information you receive.

Understanding how to integrate the channeled wisdom into your everyday life is an equally important part of channeling mastery. Receiving higher guidance is valuable only to the extent that it creates positive transformation in your consciousness, actions, and daily life.

After channeling sessions, take time to reflect on how the information applies to your current situation. What have you learned? What specific steps can you take to embody this wisdom? What patterns or beliefs might you need to shift in light of what you've received?

Creating action plans based on channeled information helps many of my students, enabling them to translate their spiritual insights into concrete practices or life changes. This bridges the gap between receiving the wisdom and actually living it, which is ultimately the purpose of all spiritual work. You're meant to do something with the information, so as long as it comes from a place of love, not harm.

The goal isn't just to access impressive information from up above - it's to bring that bright light and understanding into your physical existence, where it can create meaningful change and ripple outwards.

You may feel called to share your gift with others. Your confidence will grow. Advanced channeling mastery comes with great responsibility. Know that if you choose this path, remember that serving as a channel for others requires impeccable ethics, continuous refinement of your abilities, and honest recognition of your limitations. Try by channeling for trusted friends who can provide constructive feedback, and consider mentorship from experienced channelers before offering this service more broadly.

Whether you channel primarily for your own growth or eventually share this gift with others, the journey of developing these abilities offers immeasurable rewards. The line that separates your human form from your spiritual higher self will begin to blur. You'll find yourself living increasingly resilient as a clear channel for divine intelligence, expressing this light naturally through your very presence, words, and actions. I always check in with my spirit guides to help me with my day. Whenever I have a doubt, I will pause to feel into my own senses and trust what I am feeling. This is how we align our spiritual selves with our human selves.

This is the ultimate goal of all intuitive and channeling development - not to access extraordinary abilities for their own sake, but to become an ever-clearer vessel for the wisdom, love, and creative power that constitute your truest nature.

Trust that every practice, every moment of openness to wisdom, and even each apparent failure or confusion serve this deeper purpose of awakening the channel of light that you truly are.

The practices and techniques shared in this chapter represent gateways to an expanded consciousness, but the journey itself is uniquely yours. Honor your own unique process and celebrate each step of growth. Remember that developing intuition and channeling abilities is not a linear path but a spiral of ever-deepening awareness. Make it fun. Have fun. If you are trying too hard, pause or take a few deep breaths.

Your capacity to receive and transmit higher wisdom will continue to evolve throughout your lifetime, guided by the very intelligence you are learning to channel more consciously.

As you integrate these practices into your daily life, you become part of an ancient, cosmic, and ongoing tradition of humans who have served as guides and translators between dimensions of consciousness, bringing the light of higher understanding through you to shine into our collective human journey.

This powerful and sacred work connects you with countless other intuitives and spiritualists across time and space who have dedicated themselves to becoming clear channels for divine wisdom, contributing to the collective healing of the world. Your personal development not only serves your personal evolution but also contributes to an awakening of consciousness here on this planet, truly embodying what it means to be a channel of light.

Have fun. Play. Be open.
I want to thank you for being who you are.

Chapter 7: Meditation: The Gateway to Inner Realms

Although I don't remember much about my childhood, I have many memories of my grandmother at her apartment in Hong Kong. My grandfather was there at that time, but my connection with my grandmother was and is deeper. With her, I learned the simplest forms of Zen meditation available to anyone.

The apartment didn't have soft couches or sofas; instead, it was adorned with wooden stools and benches that could be easily moved around the small space.

Seated on a small wooden stool across from my grandmother, she asked me to firmly plant my feet on the ground, straightening my spine as if a thread pulled from the top of my head up toward the ceiling and into the heavens.

"Tuck your chin in just a little bit. Put the tip of your tongue up against the roof of your mouth," she would instruct. "This connects the energy from the heavens above down into your body. There is a hollow cavity behind your nose and eyes that needs to be connected. This allows the chi (energy) to flow completely through you."

This small detail is part of a tradition that many meditation practitioners have honored for thousands of years.

"With each breath in and out, you're going to count for one. On the second set of in and out, you're going to count for two. Then, three. Four. Five. Six. Seven. Eight. Nine and Ten. The trick here is that we are also going to observe what comes up in the mind. If your mind starts to float away into other thoughts, you'll need to bring it back to one. Do you understand, San-Ya?"

Her technique couldn't have been simpler. Breathe in, count one, breathe out. Breathe in, count two, breathe out. Continue until you reach ten, then start again at one. Make sure to notice where your mind goes. Reset if you need to. This is the practice of deepening your stillness and inner peace.

"When your thoughts drift away - and they will," my grandmother would say, "just notice it without judgment, and just start again at one. It's okay to mess up."

Even today in my practice, I still teach the same technique that my grandmother taught me. Many of my students are pleasantly surprised when their minds are literally cleared in under ten minutes.

Non-judgment forms the foundation of any meditation practice, and also of my personal approach to life. Meditation is not about beating yourself up; rather, it is about learning to observe what comes up when you meditate.

If you find yourself beating yourself up with shame or guilt, then the way you treat yourself also needs healing attention. Keep breathing and counting. Just notice the thoughts, but don't become them.

We easily 'become' our thoughts because the difference between you and your mind is so deeply intertwined. But, what if you could learn to separate the most wanderous part of you and tame it? This is how meditation can help you learn to accept yourself, become more authentic, and not let your thoughts define you.

My grandmother emphasized and taught something else that many Western and Zen meditation teachers overlook - allowing body movement during meditation. Traditional Zen meditation asks that you sit as still as possible, pushing beyond the desire to fidget, scratch your face, or open your eyes.

That said, my grandmother's techniques encourage natural

movement of the body. "Once you've started your practice, you might feel tension or an energy rise within you. If you feel your body wanting to sway side to side slowly, lean forward or backward, or rotate in circles, just let your body move," she would say. "The energy is awakening and rising within you. It just needs to move and sway through you so that it can be released. Notice how the mind responds to the meditation, the breathing, and how your body feels. Just be open."

I distinctly remember the first few times I sat on those wooden stools in my grandmother's temple, moving and swaying side to side in a gentle rocking motion, dropping my head forward and back. Sometimes my arms would rise up and fall to my sides.

My first instinct was to control the movement - to sit as still as possible. My grandmother would watch over my meditation practice and gently tap my shoulder or leg, reminding me to soften my body and let it flow. If I were squinting my eyes too hard, she'd ask me to relax. Over time, I surrender to each moment and breath, allowing the energy to spiral or uncoil within me, as if releasing an invisible wound-up coiled spring from its tension.

Every weekend, my family and I practiced this meditation. One particular weekend, my grandmother joked that I had learned enough to teach a class. The temple was filled with adults eager to pay their respects to the Buddhas and Bodhisattvas, as well as a thirty-minute meditation practice to clear their energies.

Confident and courageous, unwilling to be mocked or teased by my entire family, I went ahead and taught my first meditation class to a group of adults at just 8 years old. I knew the rules...

Sit up straight.

Uncross your legs and make sure they are planted firmly on the ground. Imagine an energy connecting to the heavens above and flowing back down into your body.

Connect the tip of your tongue to the roof of your mouth.

Tuck your chin down.

Relax your body.

If you need to move and sway, you can do that.

Relax your face.

Place your hands on your knees.

Now, let's begin to breathe in and out, counting one, two, and three...

It was a huge success, and my family was proud of me. I was beyond stoked and smiled for days on end.

A few years later, at the Buddhist monastery, this foundational meditation practice expanded into more extensive practices. The monks and nuns taught us that counting the breath was just a starting point - training wheels for the mind. Eventually, they encouraged us to let go of the counting altogether and simply observe the breath moving naturally in and out, while allowing thoughts to pass through our awareness like clouds drifting across the sky.

"Meditation is not about emptying the mind," Heng Sure Shr, a senior monk, explained. "It is about observing the mind without becoming a hostage to it."

This distinction changed my understanding.

The goal isn't about achieving a perfect state of thoughtlessness (which can seem like an impossible task that leads many people to become frustrated and eventually abandon meditation altogether). Instead, what we aspire to is witnessing our own thoughts without controlling them, creating space and separation in our consciousness to allow deep, powerful wisdom and insights to arise, or download, as they say.

For four years straight, I lived at the monastery in Northern California, full-time with my fellow boarding school classmates. I'd get to see my parents at least once a year, back in Hong Kong.

Once or twice a year at the monastery, the monks and nuns would host a multi-day Vipassana meditation retreat. People from all over the world would travel to the City of Ten Thousand Buddhas to participate, hoping to discover a slice of enlightenment. We children were allowed to participate in hour-long practices as it did not interfere with our studies.

Vipassana is an ancient Buddhist meditation practice that 'helps people see things as they are'. It involves sitting in complete silence, observing the body and mind without judgment, hoping for complete liberation of your mental mind.

My friends and I would frequently go to sit in the Buddha hall alongside hundreds of people. The lights would slowly dim, indicating that the meditation was about to begin. A few bells would chime to commence the mindful awareness. Facing the inner walls of the room, while seated in full or half lotus position, docents would walk around quietly with a long bamboo stick. They used it to gently nudge or prompt practitioners who had fallen asleep, or to offer support to those struggling with discomfort.

I didn't mind meditation at the time. However, I remember a particularly intense Vipassana session where I developed difficulty breathing, like asthma. Taking deep and long breaths, I struggled to find my slice of stillness. My breathing became labored, and no matter how I tried to focus on other parts of my body, the discomfort demanded my attention.

Remembering what my grandmother had told me - to allow the energy to flow through me. She'd say, "If you need to move, then move." And so I started swaying in small circles, uncoiling the pent-up energy that was causing me to suffer.

A docent came over and tapped me on the shoulder with the bamboo stick, gently whispering in my ear to be still. I just couldn't because the tension within me was too great.

Eventually, I quietly got up to go to the restroom, feeling defeated and lightheaded. What happened next taught me an important lesson about allowing the energy to flow through you during meditation.

I bent over the bathroom sink to blow my nose with running water, only to reveal the bloodiest, nastiest, and longest strand of mucus being released from my sinuses. It was more than what I thought was physically possible. The relief was almost immediate, but more importantly, it was my realization that my body was literally expelling what no longer served me. The focused breathing and energetic movement of my practice had triggered a physical expulsion of my asthma symptoms that ordinary breathing had not accomplished.

This personal experience helped me understand that meditation works on multiple levels at the same time. While many of us often focus on its mental and spiritual benefits, the practice also helps with profound physical healing and energetic clearing. The body, mind, and spirit are not separate aspects of ourselves, but an integrated system. When we meditate, we create the necessary conditions for balance and healing within ourselves, across all dimensions and timelines.

Throughout the decades, the meditation practice my grandmother taught me has not evolved, but I have begun to incorporate more expansive ways to explore consciousness itself.

In the early 2020s, while spending time on Clubhouse with my friends, I was teaching quantum meditation - a form of conscious awareness travel that allows you to explore multidimensional realms of the Universe while remaining anchored safely in your physical body.

Unlike traditional astral projection, where one experiences leaving the physical body behind, quantum meditation involves expanding your consciousness (whether real or imagined) beyond physical limitations while maintaining complete awareness and connection to your body. The process begins much like traditional meditation, starts with quieting the mind, focusing on the breath, allowing thoughts to settle, but then transitions into an active and curious journey of consciousness.

Once a deep, calm, and quiet meditative state, I guide my inner consciousness upward, visualizing my energies rising through the top of my head, floating up through the ceiling, into the trees, beyond clouds, up into the sky, and even higher into the vast Universe. While it feels entirely like a figment of your imagination (I can not stress this enough), you are practicing a deep visualization that uses the same mental faculties. It's more like using your mind's inner eye to sense and become aware of actual non-physical dimensions that exist beyond our ordinary senses.

This distinction is crucial. Yes, many people dismiss these visualizations as "just imagination," but this can cause a misunderstanding of what imagination truly is. Rather than just being an aspect for conjuring fantasies, imagination serves as our mind's inner computer dashboard with realities beyond physical perception. When properly guided through practices like quantum meditation, imagination becomes a vehicle for truly sensing, seeing, and experiencing subtle energies and higher dimensions.

For people who struggle with traditional meditation, I've found this approach to be effective, especially for entrepreneurs, executives, or high-achieving people who are used to planning, controlling, researching, or strategizing.

When working with my clients, I've noticed that many 'Type A' personalities will find Zen meditation excruciatingly painful or boring. I've always felt that way about Zen meditation, and it's no longer a secret. Our minds are hard-wired for action, exploration, and engagement. Asking to 'empty the mind' feels almost impossible and unnatural. I've seen it lead to frustration and complete abandonment of meditation altogether.

Quantum meditation offers a different path to calmness. Instead of fighting against their active minds, it encourages the use of the same mental energy and redirects it toward inner exploration. Suddenly, meditation becomes an adventure rather than a chore. One CEO client described it perfectly: "Finally, a meditation practice that feels like discovery, rather than deprivation."

The protective aspects of this meditation style can also not be overemphasized. Curiosity in the quantum realms can help you expand your consciousness, but it can also open up opportunities for malicious energies and entities to become attached to you.

Just as you wouldn't walk alone at night in an unfamiliar city without proper precautions, you shouldn't travel the Universe without appropriate protection.

Before beginning my quantum meditation, I always establish energetic protection using visualization and intention. I imagine my energy field surrounded by brilliant white-gold light that only allows positive energies to enter but deflects and repels anything that doesn't serve my highest good. I also call in my spirit guides, asking for protection and clarity throughout the journey. These precautions aren't based on fear, but on practical spiritual truths—the same truths that remind us to lock our doors at night while still welcoming friends into our homes.

Far beyond what most people can imagine, quantum meditation allows you to explore different dimensions of consciousness. With regular practice, you can learn to visit distinct realms, each offering unique experiences and teachings. These realms are widely referenced in spiritual traditions, energy work, and consciousness studies. Here are some of these fascinating dimensions:

The Etheric Realm – Think of this as the energy layer closest to our physical world. It's like a blueprint containing the energy patterns for everything that exists physically—from your body to buildings to nature. When you sense someone's aura or feel the energy of a tree, you're tapping into this realm. Healers frequently work here, detecting energy blockages and clearing them before they turn into physical problems. This layer is also described in many ancient systems, including Eastern medicine, as the subtle body just beyond the physical.

The Astral Realm – A shifting, dreamlike dimension that responds to human emotions and thoughts. Your feelings and imagination literally create the landscape here - fear creates dark zones, while love and joy manifest as beautiful gardens or healing temples. This realm helps you understand your emotional patterns and receive insights through symbolic experiences, much like how dreams can reveal deeper truths about yourself. Many traditions refer to this as the plane of the soul or the emotional body, which can be accessed in dreams, meditations, and out-of-body states.

The Mental Realm – This is where ideas take on actual form. Imagine a vast library where thoughts and concepts exist as tangible structures you can explore. In this dimension, you can study subjects by connecting directly with pure knowledge rather than just reading about facts. Many inventors and artists accidentally tap into this realm when they receive sudden flashes of inspiration or breakthrough ideas. Some mystics and philosophers have referred to this as the domain of the universal mind or collective intelligence.

The Cosmic Realm – My personal favorite! This is the expansive universe beyond Earth, teeming with different civilizations and forms of intelligence. Here you'll find beings made of light who communicate through pure thought, advanced technologies that seem like magic, and wisdom councils where evolved beings gather to guide universal development. You might visit star systems, explore interdimensional gateways, or access cosmic libraries containing knowledge far beyond human understanding. While not verifiable by science, these types of experiences are widely reported in starseed journeys, channeling, and deep altered-state meditation.

The Causal Realm – The most refined dimension, where you can see the underlying patterns that create reality itself. This is where past, present, and future exist simultaneously, allowing you to understand how actions create ripple effects across time and space. Visiting this realm brings deep insights about life's bigger purpose and the spiritual laws that shape our existence. In Vedantic and esoteric traditions, this realm is also known as the seed level of consciousness—the origin point from which everything becomes form.

The Time Realm - This realm isn't about clocks or calendars - it's about experiencing time as a dimension rather than a sequence. In this space, time feels fluid. Past, present, parallel, and future can be accessed like rooms in a house rather than points on a line. Some describe it as a dimension where timelines split, merge, or loop, and where you can witness your soul's journey across lifetimes. This realm allows you to understand the deeper rhythms and cycles that govern your life, and how personal and collective choices create ripple effects that extend beyond what is immediately visible. Those who access this realm often speak of receiving visions of possible futures or healing past versions of themselves by shifting something in their present. It's also where people report connecting to the "Akashic Records" - a kind of energetic archive that holds every soul's experiences, choices, and potentials across time.

Beyond these lie realms of even higher dimensions of pure

consciousness, where individual identity begins to merge with universal awareness. These realms are more difficult to describe in human language, as they transcend the structures of thought that our language is designed to express. Yet, even brief experiences of these dimensions can permanently transform one's understanding of reality and purpose.

The beauty of meditation is that it meets you exactly where you are, while offering unlimited room for growth. Whether you're a beginner simply learning to follow your breath or an advanced practitioner exploring cosmic dimensions, the practice continues to unfold new insights and possibilities. This is why I emphasize that there is no "failure" in meditation - every meditation session serves as an opportunity to further your practice, even if your mind feels especially active or resistant.

For those just starting with a new meditation practice, consistency matters far more than duration. Five minutes a day will transform your relationship with your mind more effectively than an hour once a week while emotionally beating yourself up. Start where you are, with what feels manageable, and allow the practice to naturally expand as your capacity grows.

Your physical environment for meditation also deserves thoughtful attention. Create a space in your home where you can feel safe and dedicated to your practice, even if it's just a corner with a cushion and perhaps a small altar with objects that hold meaning for you. Keep this space clean and free from distractions. Over time, the energy of your practice will accumulate in this area, making it easier to enter meditative states when you return to it.

Equal importance should be given to physical comfort, though this doesn't necessarily mean forcing yourself to be uncomfortable. I believe you can also meditate in bed or a soft recliner (which can lead to sleep, but that's perfectly okay). The traditional meditation posture - sitting with your spine straight, either on a cushion, a pillow, on the floor in half or full lotus, or a chair with your feet flat on the ground - has a physiological truth behind it. Your straight spine allows you to stay focused and aware of the energy flowing through you. This upright position allows energy to flow freely through the central channel of the body, as you possibly sway and move, while keeping you alert yet relaxed.

That said, meditation postures should be adapted to your body's needs. Physical limitations may require modifications, and that's okay, too. The key is to find a position that allows you to be comfortable enough to focus on your practice rather than on bodily discomfort, while still maintaining enough alertness to avoid falling asleep. If you do fall asleep, know that you should not shame, guilt, or judge yourself for falling asleep. Your body simply needs rest, and that's part of the process.

Awareness of your breath also forms the foundation of most meditation practices, but how we work with breath can vary widely. The simple counting method I learned from my grandmother remains one of the most accessible approaches for beginners. Another effective technique involves observing the natural rhythm of your breath without trying to control it and noting the subtle sensations at your nostrils, in your chest, or in your abdomen as you breathe.

More advanced breathing practices include alternate-nostril breathing, where you consciously direct the breath through one nostril at a time to balance the body's subtle energy channels, and extended exhale breathing, where you gradually extend the length of your exhale relative to your inhale, activating the parasympathetic nervous system and inducing deep relaxation.

Mantra meditation offers another powerful way into altered states of consciousness. A mantra is a sacred sound, word, or phrase that is repeated silently or aloud during meditation. The vibration of the mantra helps to train your brain waves to more coherent patterns while also aligning your energy with the specific qualities encoded in the sound. Traditional mantras like "Om," "So Hum," or the Gayatri Mantra carry the accumulated energy of millions of practitioners across thousands of years. One of my favorite personal mantras, which I used when healing my traumas, is "I am whole. I am great. I am loved."

Visualization practices offer yet another approach, especially helpful for those with strong visual processing or imagination. It might involve focusing on an internal image of a deity, symbol, or natural object, such as a lemon, or progressing through a guided journey, like the quantum meditation I described earlier. Visual meditations strengthen the place where your intuition exists, as the visualized images gradually become stronger beyond your conscious creation.

Body-based meditations include practices like the body scan, where you systematically move your awareness through each part of your body, noting sensations without judgment, and walking meditation, where you bring mindful awareness to the sensations and movements of walking. These approaches are especially valuable for grounding yourself in your physical reality and for people who process information primarily through kinesthetic channels.

Whatever form your meditation practice takes, the main benefits tend to emerge with consistent practice. Mental clarity develops as you learn to distinguish between essential thoughts and mental noise chatter. Emotional regulation and mental focus improve as you create space between triggering events and your responses to them. Physical health is often enhanced through reduced stress, improved sleep, and more balanced nervous system functioning.

On the spiritual level, regular meditation gradually thins the veil between ordinary and expanded consciousness. The boundaries of self become more permeable, allowing greater access to intuitive wisdom and connection with higher guidance. Synchronicities increase in daily life as your energy field becomes more coherent and attuned to the flow of universal intelligence.

Many meditators eventually experience spontaneous out-of-body journeys or astral projection during their practice. This occurs when your consciousness temporarily separates from your physical form while your body remains deeply relaxed, similar to sleep. Unlike sleep, however, you maintain full awareness throughout the experience.

These journeys often begin with distinctive sensations such as vibrations or buzzing throughout the body, sounds like ringing, rushing water, or high-pitched tones, and a feeling of floating or subtle movement. If you experience these signs during meditation, you can either gently bring your awareness back to your physical body (if the sensations create anxiety) or surrender to the process and allow your consciousness to fully separate and explore.

Should you choose to explore deeper, you'll likely find yourself being able to move around your immediate environment (in your energetic body) while observing your physical body and surroundings from a new perspective. With practice, you can learn to travel to distant locations, visit other planes of existence, dimensions, realities, and even connect with loved ones who have passed from physical life.

Please remember that safety protocols for any type of quantum meditation travel include setting clear intentions before starting your meditation, establishing energetic protection through visualization or prayer, and maintaining a discerning attitude throughout your journey. Always set an intention to return fully to your physical body at the end of your exploration, and ground yourself afterward through physical movement, eating a snack, or touching natural materials like stone or wood.

The etheric body - the energy field that interpenetrates and extends slightly beyond your physical form - serves as the intermediary between your physical body and higher subtle bodies during meditation and astral experiences. Strengthening and purifying your etheric body supports both deeper meditation and safer astral travel.

Practices that enhance the etheric body include spending time in nature, working with crystals, consuming high-vibration foods, practicing breathwork, and receiving energy healing.

You'll likely discover, with practice, that the boundaries between meditation and daily life will gradually dissolve. The presence and awareness you develop during your formal practice will begin to infuse into your ordinary activities. You might find yourself spontaneously entering meditative states while walking in nature, creating art, or even during routine tasks like washing dishes or waiting in line. This is what we are aspiring for.

Conscious and subconscious integration represents the true path of meditation, not as a separate activity you perform at specific times, but as a quality of consciousness that permeates your entire life. The inner realms accessed through meditation aren't truly separate from ordinary reality. Rather, they represent deeper dimensions of the reality we encounter every day, normally hidden by our conditioned patterns of perception and thought.

Let's be real here - you are not escaping the world through quantum meditation, but rather learning to perceive and engage with fuller dimensions. This, perhaps, is the greatest gift of a sustained meditation practice as it transforms you into a living and breathing bridge between inner and outer realms, between Heaven and Earth.

Your presence itself becomes a way through which higher consciousness can flow into the world, touching everyone and everything you encounter with the light of expanded awareness.

Chapter 8: Holistic Health and Energy Healing

I believe that the physical body is not separate from our spirituality. If anything, our body is deeply interconnected to our soul, and the way we deepen our connection with intuition. The body was never meant to be seen as something separate from your soul. You exist right now as a spiritual being in a human body that walks this Earth. This understanding guides how I help my clients achieve total health and wellness across all physical, emotional, mental, and spiritual dimensions.

Many people I work with want to focus on their intuition while neglecting their physical body. They ignore the signs their body is sending them as they try to deepen their intuitive abilities. Once I help shift this fundamental perspective, I've seen firsthand the powerful transformations that happen when people finally understand that everything is connected. There's no exception to this rule.

Back in 1998, I was formally attuned to Reiki. Reiki is a Japanese technique that uses light touch or hovering hands to help energy flow through the body. I was grateful to receive my Level 3 Reiki Master training in the Usui lineage. Some of the concepts I learned have become integral parts of the new energy healing modality I created and use today. The attunement ceremony was powerful back then - the Reiki master opened and aligned my energy channels so that I could become a clearer conduit for healing energy.

I remember feeling a surge of warmth flowing through my arms and hands. A gentle pulsing throughout my body confirmed that this energy work is real and tangible.

Initially, I practiced Reiki on myself, my animals, and the animals at the non-profit rescue I co-founded. I was pleasantly shocked by the results - my headaches disappeared, I slept better, and emotional tension melted away. The rescue animals gradually became more playful and relaxed, too. Yet, despite these positive outcomes, I had to step away from the practice because my now ex-husband mocked me for being "weird."

"You'll never be able to make a living doing that. Ha! If you can, then I'll let you quit your job," he'd smirk.

I was crushed because I knew deep down inside, I was always meant to be a healer. I believed he was right, thinking that this could never be something I do full-time. Well, he's wrong! Look at me now.

I want to tell you that this type of reaction is a huge challenge for many who are learning about spirituality and incorporating new concepts or energy healing modalities into their everyday life. The skepticism, outright mockery, and rejection from those who haven't experienced energy or intuition are downright disappointing. If you are currently going through this, I want to encourage you to keep trusting your decisions and choices - nobody can tell you how to live your life, or, for that matter, live it on your behalf.

Looking back, I see that I should have learned to trust my own instincts and beliefs. My spirit guides kept urging me to learn new modalities, but my partner wouldn't let me. You will need to learn how to protect your truth and share it only with people you trust who have your best interests at heart. I promise you, it's well worth the time and energy. Always believe in yourself.

Years later, in the early 2000s, I was led to Master Stephen Co, who taught Pranic Healing. This newer system, developed by Grandmaster

Choa Kok Sui, offered a more structured approach to energy healing, complete with specific techniques for scanning energy fields along the body, clearing blockages, and energizing areas that have been depleted. What fascinated me the most was how Choa Kok Sui had developed this method. He, with an engineering mindset, worked closely with clairvoyants who could see the energy field, allowing them to collaborate and methodically document the effects and use of different colors, hand movements, and intentions on the human energy system.

Pranic Healing opened my understanding to the power of color in energy work. Every chakra responds to different colors and frequencies. Directing specific colors with clear intention can help balance and harmonize the entire energetic system. For example, visualizing and projecting emerald green energy into the heart chakra encourages emotional healing and compassion, whereas royal blue energy directed to the throat chakra enhances clear communication and self-expression.

The system also taught precise hand movements for "sweeping" congested or stagnant energy from the field and directing new, fresh, and vibrant energy to areas that are not feeling good. These are carefully designed movements based on the observed flow of energy through and around the body. This methodical approach made sense to my analytical mind, allowing me to understand the difference between intuitive energy and the practical ways to heal chakras.

When I work with clients, I often start by clairvoyantly examining their overall chakra system, tuning into each chakra to understand where any blocks, leaks, or tears might be affecting their physical and emotional well-being. Each chakra will tell a very unique story and hold its own truths. Remember, chakras are not separate from the physical body - they interact continuously with our endocrine system, nervous system, and organs behind the scenes. They exist and can affect your energy, mood, or health, even if you don't believe in them. This is why chakra imbalances can manifest as physical symptoms in corresponding body areas.

In my earlier days, I worked with a man who didn't believe in chakras or energy healing. However, he had been suffering from stagnancy in his life. No matter how hard he tried, he couldn't break free from his own imperfections and would often sabotage work relationships and even his marriage. When we got together in our session, I scanned his chakras. They were not happy that his ego and intellectual mind kept overriding his intuition.

When I tuned into his heart chakra specifically, I recall seeing a massive block - it looked like 100,000 layers of trash bags piled up over his heart chakra, as if to obscure his ability to be loved or receive love. When I took a step back to look at his overall aura, I saw what felt like hundreds of layers of old winter coats. Again, a very part of him wanted to hide. When I shared this information back with him, he started crying. Confused by his tears, he slowly explained to me that his brother had died several years back. He confessed that he thought it would have been better if he had died and that his parents deserved the better son. He felt like a failure and a waste of life in society. It was devastating to hear. Slowly, I began my energy sweeping techniques on all of his chakras, as well as his overall chakra.

"Are you ready for me to remove the hundreds of dirty winter coats that you've been carrying all this time?" I asked.

He nodded and gave me the go-ahead. After clearing his energy for 10-15 minutes, I felt a surge of energy move through my own body, indicating that the stagnant energy had been cleared. He, too, felt the shift and cried even more tears of joy. He could not explain what had happened, but knew that something profound had occurred. Today, he is a powerful business advisor who helps executives tell their own story.

I've also worked with a large number of clients whose sacral chakra imbalances have manifested as abdominal pain, digestive issues, or menstrual problems. This second chakra, located in the lower abdomen, governs creativity, emotional flow, self-love, sexuality, and our relationship with pleasure. It has an orange-ish color. When it is blocked or imbalanced, life can feel dull and mundane. They might even feel like they are not good enough. The physical symptoms may vary, but can range from stomach cramps, a feeling of heaviness, or fertility problems.

One particular case involved a client who had chronic pelvic pain that multiple medical specialists couldn't resolve. When I was scanning her energy system, I could sense a severely constricted sacral chakra with dark, stagnant energy. The chakra was throwing a tantrum, unhappy that it wasn't being able to express itself properly. Through soft conversations about her life and work, and a deep conversation with the chakra itself, we uncovered an ongoing pattern of creative suppression - she had abandoned her artistic passions years earlier to pursue a "practical" career to please her family. The physical pain was, in essence, her body's way of expressing the pain of denied creative expression.

My work with her wasn't just about energy clearing and balancing. I gave her practical ways to reintegrate creative activities and joy into her daily life. She eventually started painting again, which led to a transition into a career path that benefited from her creative gifts. I was not surprised to see and hear that the physical symptoms resolved itself. This case demonstrates a holistic approach - addressing not just the energy imbalances but also the lifestyle choices that cause and perpetuate them.

I've also seen so many fascinating patterns of energetic connections between seemingly unrelated chakras within the same person. In several cases, I have met with clients who had root chakras that were completely blocked or had been shifted into other chakras for hiding purposes. In one case, for one reason or another, the root chakra may form an unusual and impractical alliance with the throat chakra. This pattern often tells me that the person does not feel safe in this world (root chakra issue), and will also unconsciously suppress her inner voice and hold back. This can lead to other blocks in other chakras, but the primary distortion must be first fixed. I look at the link between each chakra like water pipes in a plumbing system. If the flow of the pipes are distorted, then the water (aka light) will not be able to flow through. I will need to go through each chakra to repair them, piecing them back together slowly, while having energetic conversations with the chakras and the person him/herself.

Without addressing these issues holistically, the person will continue to feel ongoing issues of chronic anxiety and emotional depletion. At the same time, they attempt to mimic safety in other ways, rather than building their own inner trust and authentic expression.

Healing these patterns requires working across multiple levels simultaneously. I will address the subconscious programming around safety, clearing and strengthening the chakras, releasing inappropriate energetic alliances, and showing the client practical ways to incorporate healthy energetic boundaries and how to speak their truth. Much like plumbing, I need to assess the overall situation and begin the repair bit by bit. This approach recognizes that our energy system, although invisible to the naked eye, reflects our entire life experience, from our subconscious beliefs and daily habits to our divine spiritual connection.

Physical health and spiritual development are a two-way street, not a one-way street. Just as spiritual practices can promote physical healing, caring for the physical body creates a stronger channel for spiritual energies. This is why I also emphasize the importance of nutrition, movement, rest, and environmental factors alongside energy work, shadow healing, and spiritual practice.

I have had clients come to me feeling foggy and depleted. When I remote view into their chakras, I can tell that they are drained. It feels sluggish and slow. But when I remote view deeper into their bloodstreams, cells, and organs, I might find dehydration, a lack of nutrients, or that the body (or chakra) is demanding deep and nourishing rest.

What I've learned over the years is that diet plays a huge role in both your physical health and spiritual well-being. Foods that are grown in healthy soil, prepared with loving intentions, and eaten mindfully don't just give us nutrients - they transfer their life force energy to our physical system. Conversely, heavily processed foods grown with chemicals and eaten while we are distracted or stressed might fill our bellies, but they can really deplete our energy field.

I've also discovered that certain foods and eating patterns can help support your energy work and spiritual practice. Foods with high water content - think fresh fruits and veggies - seem to conduct energy way more efficiently than dense, dry foods. And here's something interesting: eating lighter meals around times when you're going to meditate or do energy healing helps. Why? Because more of your blood flow goes to your brain and energy centers instead of being completely focused on digesting heavy food. But here's a fun tip - if you're feeling extra floaty or disconnected from your body, eating protein, meat, tofu, or anything that makes your digestive system work longer will help ground you back into your physical self.

Periodic fasting or simply eating more can help clear out energetic congestion and heighten your spiritual sensitivity. You'll find this truth in spiritual traditions all around the world, which use fasting as part of their practice. But please, don't starve yourself thinking it will make you more enlightened!

I've noticed that many intuitive and spiritual practitioners find that reducing or removing animal products can increase their sensitivity to subtle energies and help with clearer channeling. But for me? The opposite is true. I actually need meat protein to keep myself grounded and prevent my consciousness from floating away. The key here is to feel into what's right for YOUR body. Yes, moral principles matter, but I want you to tune into your own vibrational compatibility and do what feels right for you.

I've also worked with people whose specific body constitution requires animal protein to maintain grounding and physical strength so they can do their spiritual work effectively. There isn't a one-size-fits-all approach here. Figuring out what your body uniquely needs requires paying attention to both your physical feedback and energy testing.

Beyond what you eat, how you move your body has a significant influence on both your physical health and energy flow. Systems like yoga, qigong, and tai chi were specifically created to balance and direct subtle energies while also strengthening your physical body. These "moving meditations" help clear energy blockages, get your life force energy flowing, and create better harmony between your physical and subtle bodies.

Even regular exercise can benefit your energy work when you bring awareness to it. Cardio gets your energy circulating throughout your whole system. Strength training enhances your body's electromagnetic field. And flexibility work releases tension patterns that can trap stagnant energy. The magic ingredient is being mindfully present during any movement practice. That's what turns exercise from just physical exertion into something that integrates your body, energy, and awareness all at once.

Rest and recovery are just as important as anything else. During deep sleep, your energy body naturally repairs and rebalances itself. It releases all the stress you've accumulated and processes the energetic input from everything you experienced that day. Your spirit guides might even do some healing or system upgrades while you're sleeping - that's one reason why you sometimes wake up feeling more balanced and clear. If you're not getting enough sleep or refusing to let yourself rest, it doesn't just affect your brain function and physical health. It weakens your energetic integrity, making you more likely to pick up other people's energies and less effective at maintaining your own field.

Getting quality sleep involves both physical factors (a dark room, quiet space, and a comfortable temperature) and energetic hygiene. Many people find it super helpful to do a brief energy clearing practice before bed - you might imagine all the day's accumulated energies being released into the Earth, or picture yourself surrounded by cleansing white or violet light. This helps prevent you from processing other people's energies while you sleep and can lead to even deeper, more restorative rest.

Our environments impact our energetic well-being, too. Our homes, cars, and workspaces all hold energetic imprints of the activities, emotions, and intentions that have been expressed there. Regularly clearing your living spaces of energy - whether through smudging with sage or sweetgrass, using bells or singing bowls for sound clearing, or practicing visualization - helps create a supportive space for both your physical health and spiritual development.

Electronic devices and electromagnetic fields can be quite challenging for energy-sensitive people in our modern world. These technologies emit frequencies that can disrupt our subtle energy field, potentially causing fatigue, brain fog, and a reduction in intuitive clarity. You might want to create device-free zones in your home, especially in your bedroom. You can also practice grounding after using your computer or place crystals like black tourmaline, clear quartz, rose quartz, or shungite near your electronics to help harmonize their energy output.

Speaking of crystals - they're my favorite form of energy to work with! These naturally formed mineral structures offer such powerful support in energy healing work. Every type of crystal vibrates at its own specific frequency that can help lift our energies into greater happiness, clarity, and alignment. For example, amethyst's energy frequency supports spiritual heart-based connection and intuitive development, while hematite's denser vibration helps with grounding and physical stability.

When I work with crystals, I intuitively choose stones whose properties address specific imbalances or support particular aspects of someone's development. In my in-person retreats and experiences, I might combine multiple healing modalities to address each client's needs more comprehensively. This could include calling in the highest frequency spiritual teams, doing hands-off energy work to clear blockages (I never physically touch my clients), placing specific crystals to maintain certain frequencies, using sound therapy to break up stagnant patterns, and guiding visualizations to get the client actively participating in their healing process. I also incorporate deep conversations throughout because they help the intellectual mind integrate these new truths and create inner balance.

My work with the chakra system has been greatly enhanced by understanding how these energy centers connect not just to physical health but also to the spiritual guidance framework I talked about in earlier chapters. The chakras serve as interfaces between different levels of consciousness, ranging from dense physical awareness to the most expanded spiritual states.

Working with the entire spectrum of chakras - from the root

chakra's connection to physical survival to the crown chakra's connection to universal consciousness - creates a much more complete healing approach than focusing only on either physical or spiritual dimensions.

I've seen so many spiritual seekers get fixated on developing just their upper chakras - heart, throat, third eye, and crown - while completely ignoring the real power of their lower chakras. This chakra discrimination can create an imbalance where your spiritual connection might be strong, but your practical manifestation and physical well-being suffer.

People who focus only on material success and physical health without any spiritual development might have really strong lower chakras but limited access to spiritual guidance, inspiration, creativity, and the expanded awareness that comes through the upper centers.

Holistic healing aims to develop and balance your entire system, creating a clear channel for energy to flow from the highest spiritual levels all the way into physical manifestation. This balanced development helps you be both spiritually connected and function effectively in the material world - true embodied spirituality, rather than escapism or pure materialism.

Quantum healing represents an evolution in energy medicine that brings together insights from both quantum physics and ancient spiritual wisdom. This approach recognizes that healing can happen instantaneously when consciousness shifts at fundamental levels - it doesn't always have to be a gradual, step-by-step process. The quantum perspective understands that energy and matter are interchangeable, that consciousness affects physical reality, and that healing information can transfer beyond the limitations of physical distance.

My exploration of different spiritual modalities really took off in the late 2000s when I joined an in-person channeling group in Culver City. While the group was originally focused on developing channeling abilities, this practice opened unexpected doors to my psychic energy healing capabilities.

During one of our monthly in-person sessions, while everyone else was meditating with serious faces, I decided to experiment with what I playfully refer to as my "psychic VR goggles" - a visualization technique where I imagine wearing special psychic glasses that let me see energy and non-physical beings.

Looking around the host's home through my imaginary goggles, I was surprised to see small, gnome-like beings scurrying about the house and property. After the meditation, when the host opened the floor for conversation and sharing, I sheepishly asked if she had any gnomes around her house. Her eyes went wide with excitement as she confirmed my vision even before answering, "Yes! How did you know?"

This experience validated my clairvoyant abilities and gave me the confidence to keep developing my perception of psychic realms, energies, and beings.

As my confidence grew, I discovered I could not only see energies but also receive specific instructions about how to work with them for healing. My first consistent spirit guide, Raquel, began offering insights about specific energy patterns in people around me and suggesting ways to help restore balance. For years, I tried researching this guide, assuming "Raquel" must be some known spiritual figure, but I found nothing. This uncertainty made me deeply question whether my experiences were real.

Eventually, I expanded my channeling practice to include more widely recognized beings, such as Archangel Michael, Gabriel, and Raphael. These connections provided additional validation because the information I received consistently proved helpful and accurate. I could also see their outline, shape, clothing, and sandals. When I looked them up on the internet, it confirmed my clairvoyance.

The archangels offered specific healing protocols designed to meet each individual's needs, often involving combinations of color, sound, and intention to create quantum healing at the cellular and energetic levels. This is why I recommend working with higher-frequency beings, rather than just spirit guides, because it helps build trust and confidence within yourself.

What's particularly fascinating about quantum energy healing is how fast and efficient it is. Unlike some traditional approaches that may require multiple sessions to gradually shift an energy pattern, quantum approaches can sometimes create an instantaneous transformation when you accurately identify and address the root cause of an imbalance. This doesn't make gentler, progressive approaches less valuable - it just means different situations call for different methods, and some conditions genuinely benefit from gradual integration of healing.

Vibrational healing represents another powerful dimension of energy medicine, using sound, light, and specific frequencies to restore harmony to the human energy system. Everything in existence vibrates at specific frequencies - from dense physical matter that vibrates relatively slowly to pure consciousness that vibrates at extremely high rates. Health can be understood as your body and energy field vibrating at their optimal, most aligned frequencies. Disease or imbalance, on the other hand, involves disrupted, chaotic, or sluggish vibrational patterns.

Sound healing works directly with these vibrational medicine principles, using instruments like singing bowls, tuning forks, drums, and the human voice to introduce resonant frequencies that help restructure disharmonious patterns. Each chakra resonates with specific sound frequencies, including both musical notes and vowel sounds. For example, the heart chakra responds to the note F and the vowel sound "ay" (as in "day"). Introducing these precise frequencies helps restore the chakra to its optimal functioning.

Crystal singing bowls offer particularly pure tonal qualities for balancing the chakras. Made from crystalline quartz or other gemstones, these bowls produce sustained tones with minimal extra overtones, allowing the vibrational pattern to work more directly on specific energy centers. Tibetan metal singing bowls, on the other hand, produce complex harmonic patterns that affect your energy field more holistically, often helping to integrate the functioning of multiple centers at once.

Speaking of sound tools, I recently started playing with solfeggio tuning forks and have had amazing success with them - they've helped lift my frequencies, heal sore muscles, and even help me sleep better!

Voice toning - using your voice to create sustained vowel sounds or songs directed to specific energy centers - is one of the most accessible and powerful sound healing practices. Your voice carries your unique vibration and intention, creating a personalized healing tool that's always available to you. Simple practices, like sounding a long "ooo" (as in "moon") directed to your throat chakra, can help clear communication blockages. A deep "ah" sound, directed to your heart, supports emotional release and opening.

Light therapy or PEMF devices offer another avenue of vibrational healing, using specific wavelengths of the electromagnetic spectrum to influence cellular function and energy patterns. While traditional light therapy often uses full-spectrum light to address things like seasonal affective disorder, more targeted approaches include colored light therapy (chromotherapy) and laser or LED applications for specific healing purposes.

The therapeutic use of color builds on the understanding that different wavelengths of visible light affect our biological systems in specific ways. Red light (with its longer wavelength) tends to stimulate and activate, while blue light (with a shorter wavelength) generally calms and cools. Green light, sitting in the middle of the visible spectrum, promotes balance and regeneration. These effects happen not just psychologically but biophysically, influencing cellular function, hormone production, and nervous system activity.

I often incorporate colored light visualization in meditations, guiding clients to imagine specific colors filling areas of imbalance or entire energy centers. This approach combines the vibrational quality of the color with the client's consciousness and intention, creating a powerful healing synergy. While it might seem simple, these visualizations can create real, measurable shifts in physical symptoms and emotional states.

Frequency-specific healing takes vibrational medicine into even more precise territory, using specific electromagnetic frequencies to address particular conditions. Research in this area has identified frequency ranges that appear to influence specific tissues, pathogens, or cellular functions. Some practitioners use devices that generate these frequencies, while others work with visualization and intention to introduce specific vibrational patterns into the energy field. Trust what feels right to you.

The effectiveness of all these approaches - from traditional Reiki to quantum healing to vibrational medicine - ultimately depends on the practitioner's clarity, presence, and connection to higher guidance. Technical knowledge of energy systems certainly helps, but the most significant healing happens when the practitioner serves as a clear channel for intelligence and love that goes beyond individual understanding.

This brings us back to the core principle of becoming a channel of light - developing ourselves as clear conduits through which healing energy and information can flow to serve others. The most effective energy healers recognize that they aren't personally generating the healing but rather aligning themselves with and directing universal healing intelligence. This humble recognition enhances rather than diminishes healing effectiveness, because it removes the limitations of the individual ego from the healing process.

Whether you're drawn to develop your healing abilities or simply want to maintain optimal health across all dimensions of your being, the principles of holistic health and energy healing offer powerful tools for your journey. By honoring the interdependence of physical health, emotional balance, energetic alignment, and spiritual connection, you create the necessary conditions for expressing yourself fully as the conscious, vibrant being you are - truly a channel of light in every aspect of your existence.

Chapter 9: Sacred Geometry and Universal Patterns

I remember playing with those little toy kaleidoscopes as a kid. You know, those long tubes you hold up to your eye that show you all these amazing patterns and colors? My fascination with kaleidoscopes continues even today because they show us something many of us sensed but didn't quite understand back then.

The Universe really does speak in patterns. Just look at the spiraling arms of galaxies, the way seeds arrange themselves in a sunflower, how trees branch out, or the delicate structure of a snowflake. These mathematical patterns are at the foundation of everything, from tiny subatomic particles to massive cosmic structures.

What spiritual traditions have always called sacred geometry, science is now confirming through quantum physics, fractal mathematics, and systems theory. The Universe is structured according to very precise geometric principles that repeat themselves at every level of existence.

Now, I know some of you might be thinking, "I'm not great at math," or "Geometry wasn't my thing in school." Don't worry! You don't need to understand mathematics to work with these patterns effectively. Your consciousness already knows how to work with them – it's built right into your very being. Just like you don't need to understand aerodynamics to appreciate the beauty of a bird in flight, you don't need to be a mathematician to work with sacred geometry.

Back in 2020, when I started spending more time on that talk app Clubhouse, I began regularly guiding people directly into the cosmic Universe through my quantum meditation techniques. As I've mentioned before, this type of quantum meditation is a form of astral traveling that's a bit different from regular astral projection. The key difference is that we stay fully lucid and awake throughout the entire experience.

Before starting any quantum meditation, I always ask everyone to suspend their expectations and let their imaginations run wild. The thing is, when you let go of physical, emotional, and mental limitations, you create space for your mind to fill with complete presence and clarity.

Through this technique, I can guide consciousness to different locations, dimensions, and timeframes, bringing back insights and wisdom from far beyond our ordinary reality.

One day, after spending hours talking with friends on Clubhouse, I closed the app and felt inspired to travel somewhere completely new during my meditation.

Instead of visiting my usual spiritual places or exploring planetary destinations like Mars or the Moon, I had this wild idea: What if I could travel back in time to witness the very beginning of everything – the moment when the Creator created Creation and even the Creator itself?

With that intention in mind, I started my quantum meditation. As my awareness expanded beyond space, time, and physical limits, I found myself floating in the Universe in that transitional space I recognize as Source or Home. But unlike my previous visits where the space was filled with light, this time I felt into the space and there was... nothing. Absolute emptiness.

In that moment, I understood I had actually traveled to a point before the Creator had created itself – before Creation had begun, before even the Creator had manifested as a distinct consciousness.

As I suspended my need to control the situation and simply allowed myself to observe, something extraordinary began to unfold.

A tiny speck of light appeared in the middle of all this nothingness, glowing faintly in the distance. This light wasn't coming from anywhere – it simply emerged, like this primordial spark of what I understood to be a rudimentary consciousness about to discover itself.

The scene before me transformed into what looked like the birth of awareness itself. The speck of light began moving slowly, as if it were discovering it could move through pure intention. At first, the movement seemed random, but soon a pattern emerged – the light was learning, exploring, and discovering that it could control its own direction and speed.

Watching this reminded me of the old Atari game 'Pong', where a simple white pixel bounces across a screen - up, down, left, and right. The light discovered it could propel itself with increasing velocity and direction, bouncing off what seemed to be the 'edges' of potential space and time.

Then a crucial discovery occurred: when moving with enough speed and intention, the light could intersect with its own trail of energy, creating a point of contact with itself.

This self-intersection led to something amazing, like an energetic mitosis where the single point of light spontaneously split into a second point of light. Consciousness had discovered how to multiply itself! From there, the process accelerated exponentially as the original awareness learned it could control multiple aspects of itself, creating increasingly complex patterns through intention.

The next stage revealed nothing less than the birth of sacred geometry and Creation. As the points of light multiplied and arranged themselves into more complex configurations, they naturally formed perfect shapes, then overlapping shapes, eventually creating the pattern known across ancient traditions as the Flower of Life – this circular geometric template that contains all other patterns and forms. Intelligence itself was being born through pattern recognition and creation.

My understanding of sacred geometry completely transformed through this experience. These patterns aren't just arbitrary human inventions or pretty designs – they're the actual templates through which consciousness creates reality at all levels. The Flower of Life, I watched being created at the dawn of existence, is the same pattern found carved into ancient temples from Egypt to China, from India to Mexico. Somehow, across time and culture, humans have always recognized and honored these fundamental patterns of creation.

Understanding these patterns is a crucial part of becoming a channel of light. When we align ourselves with universal geometric principles, we naturally become clearer conduits for divine energy. It's like tuning an instrument to the right frequency – suddenly the music flows effortlessly.

The Flower of Life deserves special attention as a master template of creation. Here's why: this pattern starts with a single circle, symbolizing unity consciousness or that first spark I witnessed in my quantum meditation. Then, additional circles of the same size are added, each centered on the circumference of existing circles, creating this perfectly balanced, infinitely expandable pattern of overlapping circles.

What makes this pattern truly remarkable is that it contains virtually all other geometric forms – the five Platonic solids (the only perfectly symmetrical three-dimensional shapes possible), the Golden Ratio, the Tree of Life, and countless other sacred forms. From this single template, infinite expressions of creation can emerge, just like the Universe creates boundless variety from a few simple fundamental principles.

The Golden Ratio (approximately 1:1.618) is another universal pattern that appears consistently throughout nature, art, and even the human body. This mathematical relationship creates proportions that people across all cultures find aesthetically pleasing. We see it in the spiral arrangement of sunflower seeds, the branching patterns of trees, the proportions of our faces, and countless other natural forms.

When consciousness is created through this ratio, a special kind of harmonious growth happens – one that can expand infinitely while maintaining perfect proportional relationships at every scale. This might explain why Renaissance artists and architects deliberately used this ratio in their works, and why we find these same proportions in structures as diverse as the Great Pyramid, the Parthenon, and the nautilus shell.

The Fibonacci sequence (where each number is the sum of the two preceding ones: 0, 1, 1, 2, 3, 5, 8, 13, 21, etc.) gives us another window into universal patterning. This sequence, which closely approximates the Golden Ratio as it progresses, appears in numerous natural phenomena, from spiral patterns in galaxies to the arrangement of leaves around a stem.

These patterns directly influence our lives, and we can consciously work with them for personal and spiritual development. Our bodies are constructed according to these same geometric principles. The DNA molecule follows a precise geometric pattern – a double helix that embodies the Golden Ratio in its proportions. Our cells arrange themselves in geometric patterns that optimize function and energy transfer.

Even our bioelectric fields form what's called a toroidal field – this donut-shaped energy pattern that surrounds and goes through our physical body.

Let me explain this toroidal field more clearly. Imagine a donut or bagel shape. Now, picture energy flowing through the center hole, around the outside, and back through the center again in a continuous loop. This circular flow pattern is called a torus or toroidal field. It's like a three-dimensional version of the infinity symbol, with energy constantly cycling through and around.

I discovered this energetic shape during a self-guided quantum meditation, when I was exploring the universe, and returned to my physical form at home. I decided to observe my energy field from a higher perspective. I was fascinated by the donut-shaped energy pattern that flowed continuously through and around my body. Confused by what I was seeing, I went online and discovered that this structure is called a toroidal field – the same pattern found in the electromagnetic field of Earth, the sun, and even galaxies.

By consciously aligning with these natural patterns, we get to experience greater harmony, health, and manifestation ability. This alignment can occur through various practices, such as meditation with sacred geometric forms, creating or surrounding yourself with art that incorporates these patterns, movement practices that trace these shapes with your body, or simply bringing awareness to these patterns as they naturally appear around you.

The Flower of Life can be used as a meditation template for harmonizing all aspects of your being. By visualizing yourself at the center of this pattern and allowing your awareness to expand through all the interconnected circles, you naturally align your energy centers and bring greater coherence to your field. This visualization practice is especially helpful when you're feeling scattered or disconnected – it restores a sense of inner order and wholeness.

Here's a simple practice you can try right now: Close your eyes and imagine yourself at the center of the Flower of Life pattern. Feel the circles expanding outward from your heart center, each one perfectly balanced and interconnected. Breathe into this pattern for a few minutes, letting your energy naturally align with its harmonious structure. Many of my clients report feeling more centered and clear after just a few minutes of this practice.

A powerful tool for manifestation work is the Golden Spiral. By visualizing your intentions moving from the center point of the spiral outward through its natural expansion, you align your creative process with universal growth patterns. This approach recognizes that manifestation usually isn't instantaneous but unfolds through a natural sequence of development, just like a plant grows according to its genetic blueprint rather than appearing fully formed.

The Platonic solids offer fascinating templates for balance and integration. Each of these five perfect three-dimensional forms corresponds to an element and aspect of being: the tetrahedron (fire) connects with will and energy, the cube (earth) with structure and stability, the octahedron (air) with thought and connectivity, the icosahedron (water) with emotion and adaptability, and the dodecahedron (ether) with spiritual essence and higher consciousness.

These universal patterns also show up in the cycles and relationships of our lives. The people who repeatedly come into your life, the situations that seem to recur in different forms, the themes that persistently appear in your dreams – these are all expressions of underlying geometric patterns operating through your life experience.

By becoming aware of these patterns, you gain the ability to work with them intentionally rather than being unconsciously pulled by them. If you notice challenging relationship patterns repeating, you can use sacred geometry to understand where in the pattern you have the opportunity to make different choices.

I had a client who kept attracting the same type of toxic romantic relationships. When we looked at her pattern through the lens of sacred geometry, she realized she was stuck in a repetitive spiral. By visualizing herself stepping out of that spiral pattern and into a new geometric flow – the Flower of Life – she was able to break the cycle. Within months, she attracted a completely different type of partner who honored and respected her.

Just as a slight adjustment to one point in the Flower of Life would change the entire subsequent pattern, small conscious choices at key moments can transform your entire life trajectory.

The toroidal field I mentioned earlier is effective for manifestation. By visualizing yourself at the center of this donut-shaped energy flow, with energy moving through your central channel and cycling back around your field, you create an energetic alignment with universal creative processes.

Intentions placed within this flow can materialize with remarkable synchronicity and minimal resistance. The toroidal pattern, once you've felt into it and become aware of it, creates a perfect balance of giving and receiving, outflow and inflow, expression and assimilation – exactly the dynamics required for sustainable creation.

The ancient principle "as above, so below" reflects the understanding that universal patterns repeat at all scales. Gothic cathedrals, Egyptian pyramids, Hindu temples, and other sacred structures around the world incorporate precise geometric proportions that mirror cosmic ratios. You can apply this same principle in your environment through arranging furniture, selecting art with the right proportions, and designing the layout of your living or working space.

But you don't need to rebuild your house to work with sacred geometry! Start small: notice the spiral pattern in your morning coffee as you stir it, appreciate the fractal patterns in the vegetables you're chopping for dinner, or observe the golden ratio proportions in flowers as you walk by. Even the way you organize your desk or arrange photos on your wall can become a conscious practice of working with these patterns. One of my students started arranging her office plants in a Fibonacci spiral pattern and reported feeling more creative and focused at work.

Perhaps the most incredible application of sacred geometry comes when you understand how consciousness itself works. My journey to witnessing the birth of the Flower of Life revealed how consciousness and geometric patterns are intimately connected.

The way consciousness organizes itself naturally follows these geometric relationships. These patterns then provide the framework through which consciousness continues to evolve and express itself.

When we work with sacred geometry through regular meditation, quantum meditation, or creative practice, we're participating in the fundamental creative process of the Universe. The same patterns I saw at the dawn of creation continue to operate through each of us, every moment. By bringing conscious awareness to these patterns, we step more fully into our role as co-creators with universal intelligence.

This understanding transforms our relationship with manifestation. Rather than trying to force outcomes through willpower alone, we can align our creative intentions with the natural geometric unfoldment patterns of the Universe. Just like a plant doesn't force itself to grow but naturally follows the geometric blueprint encoded in its seed, our creations can emerge through alignment with universal patterns rather than through struggle.

The practice of consciously working with sacred geometry also develops our pattern recognition abilities in everyday life. We begin to notice the golden spiral in how relationships develop, the Flower of Life in how communities form and interconnect, and the fractal patterns in how careers unfold over time.

This recognition brings a sense of meaningful participation and collaboration in a precisely designed cosmic realm, rather than just random existence in a chaotic Universe.

When consciousness directly perceives the geometric foundations of reality, something shifts in how we relate to our creative capacity. We begin to sense ourselves as integral parts of the universal creative process rather than isolated individuals struggling against external circumstances.

This perspective shift represents the essence of what it means to be a channel of light, recognizing that the same creative intelligence that designs galaxies and DNA molecules also flows through your awareness, available for conscious participation.

Whether you begin by meditating with the Flower of Life, noticing patterns in nature, or simply becoming aware of the sacred geometry in your everyday surroundings, you're taking steps toward aligning with the fundamental creative forces of the Universe. And that alignment is what allows us to become ever clearer channels for divine light, wisdom, and creative power to flow through us into the world.

Chapter 10: Stories of Transformation and Awakening

I've shared quite a bit about my own story, but I know you're curious about the transformations of the people I work with.
The journey of becoming a channel of light unfolds differently for each person, yet we all share a common destination - awakening to our true nature as vessels for divine wisdom, healing, and creativity.

To be a channel of light means recognizing that we aren't just physical beings who occasionally have spiritual experiences, but spiritual beings choosing to express through physical form. It means opening ourselves to become clear channels through which higher consciousness can flow into the world, bringing gifts of insight, healing, and transformation to everything we encounter.

Think of yourself as a prism of pure white light where the universe can freely express itself through you in the unique colors of your personality, talents, and experiences. You don't need special abilities or credentials - just an openness to allowing divine energy to flow through your authentic self into everyday situations.

The mission is simple: to be our most authentic selves, without any external influences.
Let me be clear about something: channels of light are just

regular people, like you and me. They're not floating above the ground in constant bliss or living isolated lives on remote mountaintops. They're your neighbors, colleagues, family members, and friends who have simply awakened to their role in lifting the collective consciousness of our planet. These people make a difference in subtle yet powerful energetic ways that help shift the frequency of Earth as a whole, lifting humanity's vibration through their presence and actions.

Being a channel of light doesn't require abandoning your current life to become a monk in Tibet or a full-time spiritual teacher. You don't even have to be intuitive, psychic, or overtly spiritual. It simply means embodying your true talents and bringing them into the world through actions aligned with your authentic purpose and passions. It means becoming the most genuine version of yourself within your existing roles and relationships.

Here are some examples of how people become channels of light in ordinary life:
- A business leader becomes a quantum leader, bringing higher consciousness to boardroom decisions
- A school teacher infuses their classroom with light that awakens curiosity and wonder in students
- A yoga teacher who helps people reconnect with their bodies and breath
- A fashion stylist helping clients express their authentic essence through personal style
- A parent raising children with awareness that nurtures their spiritual nature alongside physical development
- A healthcare worker who brings a healing presence that comforts patients beyond medical treatment
- A chef preparing food with intention and love that nourishes both bodies and spirits
- An architect designing spaces that harmonize with nature and elevate consciousness
- A customer service representative treating each interaction as sacred, bringing patience and compassion
- A writer channeling insights that help readers see themselves and

the world more clearly
- A lawyer advocating for justice while maintaining integrity and compassion for all parties
- A gardener communing with plants and earth, creating sanctuaries of peace and beauty
- An engineer solving problems with awareness of how their creations impact humanity and the planet
- A corporate manager creating team environments where employees feel valued and inspired
- A financial analyst bringing ethical awareness to investment decisions, considering social impact
- A software developer writing code with intention, creating technology that enhances human connection
- A data scientist seeking patterns that reveal deeper truths, using information for compassionate solutions

When you function as a channel of light, you allow universal intelligence to move through your own gifts and life circumstances, transforming ordinary activities into sacred contributions.

The stories that follow show how this awakening process unfolds in real lives, not as abstract theory but as lived experience through ordinary people facing both everyday challenges and extraordinary circumstances.

(Note: Some names and identifying details have been changed to respect privacy, but the essence of these transformational journeys remains intact.) Each person's path contains wisdom that might inspire aspects of your own journey toward becoming a clearer channel of light.

David's story shows how a profound crisis can awaken our deepest purpose.

When I first met David, he was a promising young athlete who had just been signed by the NFL. He was young, determined, a little bit cocky, but also deeply spiritual. He could sense energies around him and had experienced psychic phenomena since childhood. However, he didn't understand how to manage these sensitivities that would often consume him. He'd unconsciously absorb other people's emotions and energies, leaving him drained and confused about which feelings were actually his own.

We began working with psychic protection techniques - how to clear his energy field, establish healthy boundaries, and distinguish between his own emotions and those he picked up from others. We also explored connections to higher spiritual beings, rather than the random spirits and impressions he had been unconsciously channeling. David made steady progress, but his journey took a dramatic turn through circumstances no one could have predicted.

A devastating accident left David with severe third-degree burns across much of his body. When I visited him in the hospital, he was barely recognizable beneath his bandages. Yet something powerful had shifted in his consciousness. Surrounded by beeping machines and the antiseptic smell of medical equipment, David spoke with remarkable clarity about his purpose on Earth.

"It's like the fire burned away everything that wasn't really me," he told me. "I can see that I'm here to serve in a way I couldn't understand before. The football career, the fame I was chasing - it was all leading somewhere else. But this had to happen."

During his recovery, David devoted himself to deepening his spiritual connection. The practices we'd explored before took on new significance as he used them to manage both physical pain and emotional trauma. What began as tools for coping evolved into pathways for profound spiritual development.

Through months of work together, David now confidently channels cosmic wisdom directly from Source to provide guidance and support for others. His transition from NFL athlete to spiritual practitioner was necessary, offering him the experience of discipline, focus, and teamwork that became the foundation of his spiritual practice. The same determination that drove him to succeed in football now fuels his commitment to spiritual excellence. His athleticism allowed him to push physical boundaries and prepared him for exploring consciousness beyond ordinary awareness. Most importantly, the leadership qualities he developed in sports now serve him powerfully in guiding others on their spiritual journeys.

David runs a thriving spiritual practice where he helps others discover their light. Recently, he has begun studying quantum meditation techniques with me, preparing to teach others the practices that have transformed his own life.

David's journey reminds us that sometimes our most painful experiences crack us open to greater possibilities. What appeared to be a tragedy became an opportunity to embrace his true calling as a channel of light. His story isn't about denying the reality of suffering, but about finding meaning and purpose even in our darkest moments.

While David's path led to a career change, many others continue in their existing professions, bringing heightened consciousness that transforms their work from within. This integration of spiritual awareness with practical life responsibilities is illustrated by Jim's journey.

A successful CEO from the Northeast, Jim, approached life with a logical and pragmatic mindset. His business acumen had served him well in building a thriving multi-million-dollar company, and he had no intention of abandoning the business world for spiritual pursuits despite experiencing an unexpected spiritual awakening.

When Jim found me on social media, he acted on a strong intuitive pull - something quite unusual for his typically methodical approach to decision-making. During our first session, he shared how recreational marijuana use had triggered what medical professionals labeled a psychotic episode, resulting in brief hospitalization. His family was deeply concerned about his sudden shift in behavior, which included making seemingly disconnected statements and claiming to receive information from invisible sources.

As Jim described his experiences, I recognized the classic signs of a spontaneous spiritual awakening without proper foundation or guidance. I explained that the marijuana had inadvertently blasted his chakras wide open, particularly his third eye and crown, before he'd developed the energetic structure and discernment to handle the resulting influx of information and energy.

(Chakras are energy centers in the body that regulate the flow of life force. The third eye chakra, located between the eyebrows, relates to intuition and perception beyond our physical senses, while the crown chakra, at the top of the head, connects us to higher consciousness and spiritual wisdom. When these centers open too quickly without proper preparation, it can create massive confusion and overwhelm.)

"You've essentially opened a door you weren't quite ready to walk through," I told him. "But now that it's open, we can work on helping you navigate what you're experiencing rather than trying to close it again. Would that be okay?"

Our work together focused on grounding, energetic regulation, and developing discernment between genuine intuitive information and mental chatter. We also addressed integrating his emerging spiritual awareness with his role as a business leader. Rather than compartmentalizing these aspects of himself, Jim learned he could bring his intuitive insights into business decisions without using spiritual jargon, while maintaining appropriate boundaries with colleagues.

Today, Jim accesses wisdom and information from higher dimensions, the Universe, and God without requiring deep meditation states. He's developed a balanced approach to his psychic gifts and now understands that this spiritual awakening isn't meant to pull him away from his business life, but rather enhances it, bringing greater depth and meaning to his work. His leadership style has evolved to be more compassionate and visionary while remaining grounded in practical realities. His employees would describe him as more present, insightful, and authentic, rather than as someone who had undergone a dramatic personality change.

Jim represents the countless professionals who serve as channels of light within traditional career paths, bringing elevated consciousness to places and environments that desperately need it without alienating those around them with overtly spiritual language or behavior. They operate as subtle agents of transformation, shifting organizational cultures through their presence and perspective rather than through preaching.

Sometimes becoming a channel of light involves clearing energetic blockages first, as demonstrated by Elena's journey.

When Elena first contacted me, she'd already spent years and thousands of dollars seeking help from various practitioners - energy healers, psychics, and even a shaman from another country who charged her $5,000 with a strong promise to remove what she described as a "demonic attachment."

During our first session, Elena's skepticism was clear. After so many failed attempts at removing this entity, she had little reason to believe my approach would be any different. During our session, I remote-viewed into her chakra system and her home. She hadn't given me any information about where she felt the presence, but I accurately described the locations within her apartment where she'd seen or felt the strange presence. I also identified the specific areas on her body and in her energy field where the entity had attached.

"The primary attachment point is at the back of your solar plexus chakra," I told her, "which is why you feel constant drainage and lack of personal power. That's also why you can't see it - it's on the back side. There's a secondary connection at your sacral chakra, which explains the creative blocks and emotional volatility you've been experiencing."

I went on to describe where the entity was hiding in her apartment: at the dining room table, in the bathtub, under her bed, and sometimes in the closet. She gasped at how accurate I was.

Energetic interference and attachment occur when unwanted energies - whether from other people (dead or alive), entities, or even our own past traumas - disrupt our natural energy flow. These interferences can manifest as persistent emotional states, physical symptoms, or blocks in our spiritual development. Clearing these interferences means removing unwanted energies and restoring the natural flow and integrity of one's energy field.

The process of removing energetic interference involves several specific steps. First, I scan the person's entire energy field and chakra system using my clairvoyant abilities to locate all points of attachment. These often appear as dark cords, cloudiness, or foreign energy signatures. Then, I examine their living situation for lingering energy imprints, as entities often hide in specific locations.

With the attachments identified and confirmed, I begin clearing by creating a protective energy field around both of us. I use specific light frequencies and invoke spiritual assistance to dissolve the connections between the entity and the person's energy centers. This goes beyond just "cutting cords" - the work I do requires psychic precision to extract the entity's energy completely from each chakra without damaging the person's natural energy system. Finally, I seal the person's aura and chakras with protective light and give them specific practices to maintain their energetic boundaries. This comprehensive approach ensures the entity can't reattach and prevents new interferences from forming.

As I guided Elena through the clearing process, I gently pulled out all the negative energy from her apartment. From there, I had a stern conversation with the spirit, telling it that it was no longer welcome and had no business attaching itself to Elena. I went on to remove the psychic attachments directly in her chakras and worked until I could sense the entity being completely removed.

Elena contacted me thirty days later, somewhat surprised to report that she'd experienced no more disturbances. It had worked almost immediately, but she wanted to be 100% sure it was gone. Even months later, she confirmed that the clearing had indeed been permanent - something no other practitioner had accomplished despite more elaborate and expensive interventions.

With the energetic interference removed, Elena could finally progress in her own spiritual development. The constant energy drain had been blocking her natural abilities, but once cleared, she began experiencing her own intuitive openings and developing a genuine connection to higher guidance. What's particularly noteworthy about Elena's story is that she didn't change careers or make dramatic external life changes. Instead, she brought her newfound energy and clarity into her existing relationships and work.

Her story reminds us that sometimes the most profound service we can offer is simply showing up as our whole, unobstructed selves. By clearing the energetic interference that had dimmed her natural light, Elena became an even more powerful presence in every environment she entered. Her light affected others without her having to consciously try to heal or change them.

This natural influence represents how many channels of light operate in the world. They don't necessarily announce themselves as spiritual beings or healers - they simply embody a higher frequency that naturally elevates those around them. Their clear energy field creates a resonance that helps others access their own innate spiritual connection. This unspoken transmission often accomplishes more than deliberate teaching or healing work.

Katherine's experience illustrates how sometimes we stand in our own way.

As a dedicated school teacher, Katherine had been exploring spirituality and intuition for years, even investing in a year-long channeling program with another coach. Despite her sincere efforts and financial investment, something continued blocking her progress.

Katherine reached out to me to help her understand what was holding her back. During our first session, I used my clairvoyant abilities to look at her chakra system and connect with her spiritual team. What I discovered surprised us both - Katherine wasn't actually blocked in the traditional sense. Her channel was already open, but her expectations about what channeling should look and feel like were preventing her from recognizing and trusting the information coming through. Her spirit guides told me this loud and clear.

Her guides gave me clear instructions to tell her: She needed to give herself permission to trust the subtle, quiet voice of intuition she'd already been hearing, rather than waiting for the dramatic, trance-like state she'd been expecting. With this understanding and some simple adjustments to her approach, transformation was nearly instantaneous. We channeled Mary Magdalene within ten minutes, then Jesus right after. I was able to confirm the frequency and messages she was hearing alongside her. They had been trying to connect with her all along.

"I can't believe it was that easy," she said, tears streaming down her face. "I kept waiting for something dramatic to happen, when they were whispering to me the whole time."

Katherine's awakening transformed her teaching style in subtle ways. She didn't start teaching spiritual concepts in her classroom or make dramatic changes to her curriculum. Instead, she brought a quality of presence and intuitive responsiveness that helped her recognize and nurture each student's unique gifts. She became more attuned to the emotional and energetic needs in her classroom, creating an environment where children felt truly seen and supported.

Her students' parents began noticing differences - children who had struggled with learning or behavior showed remarkable improvement. Children who had been withdrawn became more expressive and engaged. When asked what had changed in her teaching approach, Katherine struggled to articulate specific techniques or methods. The transformation came not from what she did, but from who she had become—a clearer channel through which wisdom, compassion, and creative inspiration could flow.

Katherine represents the many channels of light working within our educational systems, bringing higher consciousness to the development of young minds without necessarily teaching overtly spiritual ways. Their influence shapes the next generation in ways that statistics can't measure but that ripple forward through time, affecting the collective consciousness for decades to come.

For Marcus, a corporate executive with a massive list of business experience, the journey to becoming a channel of light required bridging the worlds of pragmatic leadership and spiritual awareness.

When we began working together, Marcus had conducted extensive intellectual research into spiritual concepts but struggled to move beyond conceptual understanding to direct experience and integration.

"I understand the theories," he explained during our first session. "But it's all theoretical. I can't seem to move from knowing about these things to actually experiencing them firsthand and integrating them into my life. Why do we even talk to spirit guides?"

Our work started with basic meditation practices customized to work with his analytical mind rather than trying to silence it. Instead of fighting against his mental processes, we learned to integrate this power by giving his intellectual mind specific tasks within the meditation - questions to explore, problems to solve, and places to discover from a higher perspective. This approach honored his natural strengths while expanding access to his intuitive wisdom.

Over time and with added curiosity, I taught Marcus how to remote view. He easily accessed information beyond his physical senses, and I would confirm it by remote viewing alongside him. Later, he began receiving clear spiritual guidance from higher frequencies who specialized in leadership and organizational development.

Marcus now works closely with his spirit guides and channels information without needing formal meditation. Furthermore, he has integrated this awareness into his leadership style, inspiring those around him to connect with their own inner guidance.

"The greatest revelation," Marcus shared recently, "is learning that spirituality doesn't actually demand that I abandon my intellectual faculties and business abilities - it adds to them by giving me access to information and perspectives beyond what my rational mind alone could generate."

Marcus continues to lead his organization, making strategic decisions and navigating complex business challenges. But now, he does so with expanded awareness that considers not just profit margins and market trends but the energetic impact of corporate decisions on employees, customers, and the planet. He embodies what I call "quantum leadership" - leading from a place where intuition and higher awareness inform decisions alongside analytical data.

(Quantum leadership means applying principles from quantum physics to leadership - recognizing interconnection rather than separation, understanding how consciousness shapes reality, and accessing information beyond conventional data sources. Quantum leaders recognize that their state of authenticity and connection influences their organization's culture and results, often in ways that transcend visible cause and effect.)

Through his example, others in his organization have begun

exploring personal development, creating a corporate culture that values both analytical rigor and intuitive insight. Without explicitly teaching spiritual concepts, Marcus has become a catalyst for an evolution in consciousness that now affects everyone connected to his work. It's possible to transform traditionally left-brain-dominant fields from within, bringing balance and wholeness to environments that have long operated from overly logical awareness.

These varied paths to becoming channels of light share several common patterns worth noting.

First, spiritual awakening often begins with curiosity—a willingness to explore beyond the conventional understanding of reality. This openness creates the initial crack in the door through which light can enter.

Second, proper spiritual guidance can accelerate personal development and help navigate challenges that happen in real time. While spontaneous awakenings occur, having an experienced guide who can provide context, techniques, and discernment tools makes the journey smoother and more direct.

Third, consistent practice matters more than a single dramatic experience. Every person I mentioned has developed their abilities through regular application of specific techniques - whether meditation, energy work, intellectual conversation, or conscious channeling practices. The most powerful transformations don't happen overnight but through committed engagement with whatever arises.

Fourth, integration is required for sustainable growth. You can't just talk theory, you must put it into good use. Those who have successfully navigated their gifts have learned to integrate their spiritual awareness into everyday life, rather than compartmentalizing it. The objective isn't to escape ordinary reality but to bring higher awareness into every dimension of your life.

Fifth, becoming a channel of light inevitably leads to service. I don't mean just volunteer service, but rather, allowing your authentic personality and essence to serve as inspiration for others. As people develop and deepen their connections to higher consciousness, they naturally feel called to share moments, words, laughter, stories, or energy with others. The form of service varies - from being more authentically yourself to one-on-one healing work, to conscious business leadership, and beyond - but the effect ripples out the same.

Your authenticity offers the exchange of energetic wisdom and guidance for anyone feeling called to learn more about themselves. You don't have to become someone different from who you are. Instead, this path is about discovering and expressing your authentic self more fully. The channel of light has always existed within you. This journey involves removing what blocks your natural flow and learning to trust what comes through.

The transformative power of spiritual practices shared in these stories doesn't depend on extraordinary circumstances or special innate gifts for the chosen few. Each person who has stepped into their role as a channel of light began with the same fundamental human capacity for connection to a higher power, and each has deepened their connection through consistent practice and guidance.

The experiences I've shared here remind us that becoming a channel of light isn't about achieving some elevated status separate from humanity but about fulfilling our natural role in the greater Universe. We are designed to be channels through which higher wisdom, love, and creativity can flow into physical expression here on Earth. When we embrace this role, through whatever path calls to us, we not only transform our own lives but also contribute to raising the consciousness of our planet.

This contribution doesn't require dramatic actions or public recognition. Simply by clearing our own energetic blockages, aligning with our authentic purpose, and allowing higher awareness to flow through our everyday activities, we participate in the collective awakening happening on Earth right now. The energy will continue to expand on, and on, and on. Each channel of light, whether as a healer, teacher, artist, parent, business leader, or in any other capacity, adds its unique frequency, helping to create a more aligned and balanced expression of human potential.

My clients come from all walks of life - CEOs navigating major corporate decisions, celebrities managing public pressure and maintaining personal authenticity, professionals seeking greater purpose in their careers, healers developing their skills, teachers expanding their influence, and everyone in between. What draws this diverse group to my work isn't just my abilities, but how I translate complex spiritual concepts into practical, everyday language.

I've learned that people find me because I can explain energy healing in terms that make sense to their specific reality. Whether I'm working with a high-powered executive or a kindergarten teacher, I adapt my language and approach to meet them where they are. This isn't about dumbing things down - it's about making spiritual concepts accessible and immediately applicable to daily life.

The beauty of this work is that the principles remain the same regardless of someone's profession or background. A CEO can use the same energy-clearing techniques as a yoga instructor. A celebrity can develop intuitive abilities just like a stay-at-home parent. The human capacity for spiritual connection doesn't discriminate based on job titles or social status. What matters is the willingness to be authentic and the courage to trust the process of awakening.

This practical approach has allowed me to help thousands of people integrate spiritual awareness into their existing lives without requiring dramatic changes or upheaval. Because at the end of the day, becoming a channel of light isn't about escaping your current reality - it's about bringing more consciousness, clarity, and authenticity to exactly where you are right now.

Chapter 11: Integration of Science and Spirituality

Throughout this book, we've explored so many aspects of becoming a channel of light - from awakening intuition to understanding sacred geometry, from working with energy to connecting with higher guidance. You might be wondering how these spiritual concepts relate to the rational, evidence-based world many of us navigate daily. If you're like me, you may have found yourself straddling two worlds - the mystical experiences of your inner journey and the practical realities of everyday life.

The good news is that these worlds are converging in incredible ways.

What spiritual traditions have known for millennia, science is now beginning to validate and explain through its language and methods. This convergence doesn't diminish spiritual magic - instead, it enhances it and expands our understanding of how multidimensional we truly are as channels of light.

I remember sitting with a client who works as a research scientist at a prestigious university. After experiencing energetic shifts through our healing work together, she confessed that she was feeling torn between her spiritual experiences and her scientific training.

"How can I reconcile what I'm experiencing with you with what I know about biology and physics?" she asked.

This question reflects a struggle many of us face as we awaken to our spiritual nature while living in a society that often prioritizes material evidence over subjective experience.

The truth is that being a channel of light doesn't require abandoning rational thinking or scientific understanding. The latest scientific research offers fascinating insights into how and why the spiritual practices we've discussed throughout this book create such powerful transformations. Let's explore how these two approaches to understanding reality can complement and enrich each other, helping us become more integrated channels of light in all aspects of our lives.

Remember how we talked about consciousness not being confined to our brains but extending beyond physical limitations, connecting us to a vast field of awareness? Traditional science once saw consciousness as just a byproduct of brain activity - nothing more than neurons firing in particular patterns. But quantum physics has revolutionized this understanding in ways that align perfectly with spiritual wisdom.

The famous double-slit experiment in quantum physics revealed something that has mystified scientists: particles behave differently when observed than when not observed. The act of conscious observation influences how matter behaves at the quantum level. This discovery challenged the fundamental assumption that consciousness and physical reality operate independently of each other.

As the renowned physicist Max Planck put it, "I regard consciousness as fundamental. I regard matter as derivative from consciousness."

This quantum perspective mirrors what spiritual traditions have taught for thousands of years - that consciousness isn't just an afterthought of material evolution but a primary creative force in the Universe. As channels of light, we work with this understanding intuitively when we use focused intention in meditation, energy healing, or manifestation practices. The scientific validation doesn't make these practices more real, but it does offer an opening to understand that spiritual experience and rational understanding can complement each other.

I've seen this integration unfold beautifully with clients in the business world. One CEO I worked with initially approached our sessions with healthy skepticism, which I actually encourage because I want everyone to come to their conclusions. After guiding him through a few custom quantum meditations, he realized that he wanted to learn about his intuitive gifts but struggled to reconcile this interest with his analytical mind. Through our many conversations, and as he learned about quantum physics and its implications for consciousness, something clicked.

"You know, Sonya... I think I understand. I don't need to abandon logic when it comes to intuition," he realized. "I'm starting to understand that consciousness itself works with physical reality in ways that go beyond what we previously understood and seen."

This realization transformed his leadership style. Rather than seeing meditation as separate from his business activities, he began recognizing it as a practical tool for accessing expanded awareness that informed better decision-making. The quantum understanding of consciousness as a fundamental force helped him bridge his spiritual development with his professional responsibilities, making him a more integrated channel of light in the corporate world.

The neuroscience of meditation offers another fascinating bridge between spiritual practice and scientific understanding. Throughout this book, we've explored various meditation techniques for developing your abilities as a channel of light. These practices can create measurable changes in your brain that enhance your capacity to serve as a clear conduit for higher consciousness.

Brain imaging studies show that regular meditation increases gray matter in regions associated with self-awareness, compassion, and attention, while decreasing the size of the amygdala, which processes fear and stress. In essence, meditation rewires your brain to support the qualities needed to function as a clear channel of light, presence, compassion, intuitive awareness, and emotional balance.

I saw the power of meditation when working with a client who struggled with anxiety that blocked her from self-trust. Understanding the neurological basis of meditation helped her approach her practice with greater commitment and patience.

"Knowing that meditation can physically change my brain to support calm awareness has made it easier to stick with it, even if I don't see immediate results," she shared.

Over time, as her anxiety diminished, her channel opened, allowing intuitive insights, confidence, trust, and self-love to flow more freely.

This helps explain why meditation and awareness practices create such profound shifts in consciousness. When you engage in quantum meditation or other awareness practices, you're not just having subjective experiences - you're physically reconfiguring your neural networks to support expanded states of consciousness. Your brain becomes a more effective instrument for channeling light as its structure and function align with higher awareness.

The science of heart coherence reveals another important dimension of being a channel of light. We've talked about the importance of heart-centered awareness when connecting with higher guidance and engaging in energy work. Science now confirms the heart's central role in our energetic and consciousness systems.

Research from the HeartMath Institute shows that the heart generates the body's most powerful electromagnetic field, far stronger than the brain's. This field changes based on our emotional states, with positive emotions like love, gratitude, and compassion creating coherent patterns that synchronize brain activity and improve overall functioning. Moreover, this electromagnetic field extends several feet beyond our bodies, potentially affecting others nearby.

This research provides a scientific perspective on something many of you have likely experienced - the difference in energy when you're in the presence of someone whose heart field is open and joyous versus someone whose field is dark, chaotic, or constricted. As channels of light, the state of our heart energy dramatically affects the quality and clarity of what flows through us.

I remember working with an extremely gifted psychic who struggled with consistency in her readings. Sometimes the information flowed clearly, while at other times it felt blocked or confusing. As we explored heart coherence techniques, something interesting happened.

When she consciously generated feelings of appreciation and love before attempting to channel information, her accuracy and clarity improved dramatically. The science of heart coherence helped explain why - she was creating an optimal energetic state for receiving and transmitting higher frequencies of information.

For those of you developing your authentic truth and channel of light in professional settings, heart coherence offers a scientifically validated approach to enhancing your presence and impact. Take, for example, the business leader who takes a few moments to center into heart coherence before an important meeting. They're not just doing random breathing techniques - they're creating measurable changes in their electromagnetic field, starting with their heart, that can influence group dynamics and decision-making processes. The coherent heart broadcasts a higher frequency that helps elevate collective consciousness.

Now, let's turn to one of the most powerful energetic phenomena you might encounter on your journey as a channel of light - Kundalini awakening.

In spiritual traditions, particularly those from India, Kundalini is described as a serpent-like energy that normally lies dormant at the base of the spine. When awakened, this energy rises through the central channel alongside the spine, activating the chakras and eventually reaching the crown, where it can trigger profound expansions of consciousness.

I witnessed this powerful energy in action during one of my healing sessions. During this particularly intense energy healing session, I was working to realign a client's chakras when something energetically exploded. I could see each chakra awakening, opening, and turning on, appearing as bright, vivid colors.

Suddenly, without explanation, I saw a flood of energy spiral upward from her root chakra, reaching through all the chakras and extending to the top of her head and beyond. I immediately recognized that her Kundalini energy had been activated.

While this experience might sound purely mystical and metaphysical, science offers interesting parallels that help us understand what might be happening physiologically during Kundalini activation. The central nervous system, with its intricate network of nerves extending from the base of the spine to the brain, bears a striking resemblance to the traditional description of the sushumna channel, a central energy channel. The sympathetic and parasympathetic branches of the autonomic nervous system mirror the traditional ida and pingala energy channels that spiral around the central channel.

From this perspective, Kundalini awakening may involve a dramatic shift in nervous system functioning, with increased energy flow to the brain, the release of stored tension, and the activation of higher brain centers. The subjective experience of energy rising the spine could correspond to sequential activation of nerve plexuses that align closely with traditional chakra locations.

What's particularly important to understand about Kundalini is that it can be activated through various means - dedicated meditation practices, energy healing work, yoga, intense emotional experiences, physical trauma, or even recreational drugs. As I witnessed with my client, these activations can be either positive or difficult depending on the circumstances and the individual's preparation.

When Kundalini awakens gradually in someone who has been preparing their energy system through consistent spiritual practice, it can lead to profound expansions of consciousness, heightened creativity, unexplainable happiness, and accelerated spiritual development.

However, if it activates suddenly in someone who isn't energetically or psychologically prepared, it can create overwhelming experiences like unexplainable grief or depression that might be misinterpreted as psychological disorders.

This explains why some people go through spiritual awakening as a smooth, gradual process while others experience more violent awakenings that might include physical symptoms, emotional volatility, or perceptual changes that can be disorienting. As channels of light, understanding the potential physiological basis for these experiences helps us navigate them with greater awareness and appropriate support.

The field of epigenetics offers another fascinating intersection between science and our development as channels of light. Epigenetics now shows that our inner states affect which genes get expressed in our cells and which ones remain dormant.

Research demonstrates that chronic stress and negative emotional states can activate genes associated with inflammation and disease. In contrast, practices such as meditation, positive social connections, and time in nature can activate genes associated with healing and longevity. Our consciousness influences our physical body at the genetic level.

This reinforces the importance of the energy practices and mindfulness techniques we've explored. When you engage in meditation, energy clearing, or heart coherence practices, you're creating measurable changes in gene expression that support your physical body in handling higher frequencies of energy and information.

I've seen this connection between consciousness and physical health in many clients who commit to regular spiritual practice. They often experience unexpected improvements in their physical health and emotional resilience. Some have reported becoming more productive. The epigenetic research helps explain why their consciousness practices are creating biological changes that support overall well-being.

The science of biofields provides yet another bridge between spiritual understanding and scientific research. Advanced scientific instruments can now detect aspects of this field, including the electromagnetic emissions from the heart and brain that we discussed earlier.

Research at institutions like the Institute of Noetic Sciences has shown that trained practitioners can influence biological processes through intention and energy healing practices, affecting cellular growth, enzyme activity, and healing rates in ways that cannot be explained by placebo effects alone.

While science is still catching up to what energy healers have known experientially, these studies offer validation that can help bridge spiritual practice with conventional understanding.

For those of you developing healing abilities as part of your journey as a channel of light, this research provides language and context that can help you communicate what you're doing in terms that might be more accessible to those unfamiliar with energy work. Rather than having to choose between "scientific" and "spiritual" explanations, you can recognize how these perspectives complement each other in describing the multidimensional reality in which we exist.

As I reflect on how science and spirituality are converging in our understanding of what it means to be a channel of light, I'm reminded of a beautiful quote from Albert Einstein: "The most beautiful thing we can experience is the mysterious. It is the source of all true art and science."

Both the scientist and the spiritual seeker are, at heart, explorers of the mysterious - approaching the unknown with wonder, curiosity, and a desire to understand. As channels of light in the modern world, we have the privilege of drawing from both approaches, allowing them to inform and enrich each other.

The integration of scientific understanding with spiritual wisdom doesn't diminish the magic or mystery of being a channel of light. Instead, it offers a more complete picture of who we are and what we're capable of becoming. It helps us bridge the seeming divide between our spiritual experiences and our everyday lives in the material world.

Whether you're a healthcare professional incorporating energy awareness into your practice, a teacher guiding and inspiring students, a business leader bringing higher consciousness to organizational decisions, a parent raising children with both spiritual wisdom and scientific understanding, or simply someone navigating your path of awakening, this integration supports you in becoming a more whole and effective version of yourself.

Remember that you don't have to choose between being scientifically informed and spiritually awakened. The most powerful channels of light in our time will be those who can integrate these seemingly different approaches to understanding reality, embodying the truth that transcends and includes them both.

Chapter 12: Ethical Living and Universal Responsibility

The journey of becoming a channel of light naturally leads us to a profound question: How do we integrate this light into our daily lives and relationships?

As our consciousness expands and our connection to higher wisdom deepens, we feel called to live with greater integrity, compassion, and responsibility. This inner calling isn't about following extreme spiritual rules or ideals - far from it. It's more about allowing the light to naturally express itself through conscious and ethical living, and to bring service to the greater whole in whatever way feels authentic to you.

Growing up in my grandmother's Buddhist temple in Hong Kong, I was immersed in teachings about compassion and ethical responsibility long before I understood their significance. I watched how my grandmother treated everyone who came to the temple with the same respectful presence, whether they were wealthy community leaders or low-income individuals seeking guidance. She embodied the Buddhist principle that all beings deserve dignity and care simply because they exist, not because of their status or what they could offer in return.

This principle mirrors the Christian teaching that we are all created in God's image (Genesis 1:27) and therefore deserve equal respect and dignity. Whether through Buddhist compassion or Christian love, the message is similar, though you get to decide which framework resonates with your truth.

Later, during my years at the Buddhist monastery, these early lessons deepened through formal ethical teachings and daily practice. The monastery's careful emphasis on mindfulness meant bringing conscious awareness to every action, from washing dishes to speaking with others. Nothing was too mundane for spiritual attention. These early experiences instilled in me the understanding that spirituality isn't separate from everyday life but expressed through how we show up in ordinary moments.

I knew from a very young age that I couldn't inspire greatness or step into my purpose from behind monastery walls. I knew I needed to deeply integrate into my earthly existence to inspire from the ground up. This is why I've worked so hard to heal my wounds and separate myself from organized religion. But this was my path - yours might be completely different, and that's perfectly valid.

What I've discovered through my spiritual journey is that ethical living unfolds in stages. Initially, many of us are drawn to spiritual practices for personal reasons - maybe to reduce stress, find meaning, stop suffering, or develop special abilities. This self-focused personal development stage serves an important purpose in our development, much like putting on your oxygen mask before helping others in an emergency. But as our journey continues, a natural expansion of consciousness occurs. We begin to recognize the role we play in this world through our lives and feel called to embody our natural state of awareness through ethical living and service to others.

This expansion isn't something we need to force. It emerges naturally when we clear our energy fields, open our hearts, and align with higher consciousness. The more light we channel, the more we naturally want to express that light through actions that benefit the whole - you, me, and everyone. Compassion, integrity, and service become not just obligations or rules we follow, but natural expressions of who we are becoming.

The word "integrity" comes from the Latin "integer," meaning whole or complete. To live with integrity means to be undivided - to have our inner truth and our outer actions in perfect alignment. When we walk this path, integrity becomes both our practice and our protection. When we align our thoughts, words, and actions with the highest truth we know, we create a clear, unobstructed pathway for light to flow through us.

I've seen how misalignments between inner truth and outer expression create energetic blocks that limit our capacity to channel light. When we say yes while feeling no within, when we project an image that doesn't match our true feelings, when we compromise our values for external gain - each of these creates distortions in our energy field that block the flow of higher consciousness through us.

On the other hand, when we commit to radical honesty and alignment between our inner and outer worlds, something remarkable happens. Our channel clears and expands, allowing more light to flow through with less distortion. This alignment requires tremendous courage - the courage to be seen in our authentic truth even when it's uncomfortable or challenges prevailing norms.

Living with integrity doesn't mean perfection. We all have moments of misalignment and inconsistency. What matters is our commitment to noticing these gaps between our inner truth and outer expression, and gently bringing ourselves back into alignment. This ongoing practice of self-honesty and realignment constitutes the foundation of ethical living as a channel of light.

The Buddhist concept of Right Speech offers practical guidance for integrity in communication. Before speaking, we were taught to consider:

    Is it true?
    Is it necessary?
    Is it kind?
    Is this the right time?

Similarly, in Christian tradition, Ephesians 4:15 speaks of

"speaking the truth in love," while James 1:19 advises us to be "quick to listen, slow to speak." These various traditions offer frameworks that you can explore and adapt to your spiritual understanding. The key is finding what genuinely resonates with your inner truth.

Integrity also extends to how we work with our spiritual gifts and abilities. As my intuitive abilities strengthened and my energy sensitivity increased, I encountered situations where I could use these gifts in ways that benefited myself at others' expense. The temptation to manipulate, to look into others' energy fields without permission, or to use spiritual insights to control rather than serve can arise for anyone.

I remember when I was learning how to remote view - the practice of attempting to telepathically perceive information about a distant or hidden subject. I'd spend time practicing by locating my cats within specific areas of the house without getting up. I'd practice finding the keys I had misplaced. I'd practice going through my office desk to look at what was laid out on the table. Eventually, I realized that I could easily look into private spaces or energy fields. I was careful to apply morals and ethics around 'snooping', but would never do anything without someone's knowledge or consent. The power of remote viewing both excited and sobered me. Every time a client would ask me to 'look into' something, I'd have to establish clear ethical boundaries for myself and the person I'm looking into - never using these abilities for personal gain, manipulation, or to intrude on someone's privacy, but only in service and with appropriate permission.

Being able to remote view comes with a lot of excitement about the limitless possibilities. The self-regulation I apply to my abilities doesn't come from fear of punishment but from understanding that the misuse of spiritual gifts distorts our own channel of light. When we use our gifts in alignment with universal principles of respect, compassion, and service, we become clearer conduits for light. When we misuse them, we create static and interference in our channel, regardless of whether anyone else is aware of what we've done.

This aligns with the Christian teaching about spiritual gifts, which emphasizes that gifts are given for the common good, not personal gain. But ultimately, you must develop your ethical framework in relation to spiritual abilities.

If integrity creates the clear structure of our channel, compassion provides its heart-centered essence. Compassion - the ability to sense others' suffering coupled with the genuine desire to alleviate it - represents one of the highest frequencies of consciousness we can channel. When we operate from true compassion, we become conduits for healing frequencies that touch everyone we encounter.

The Buddhist teachings in my childhood emphasized compassion (Karuna) as the natural expression of wisdom and truth. When we truly see the interconnected nature of all life, compassion arises spontaneously. It's not something we need to manufacture or force, but something that flows naturally when we recognize others as extensions of ourselves.

Christian teachings offer similar wisdom through the concept of Agape - unconditional love that seeks the highest good for others. Jesus taught to "love your neighbor as yourself," pointing to the same interconnectedness that Buddhist teachings also emphasize.

Compassion differs from sympathy or pity, which creates a distinct separation between the one who suffers and the one who observes. True compassion comes from the recognition of our fundamental Oneness with everyone in the world - the understanding that other people's suffering and joy are not separate from our own. Perhaps a friend or someone you know is going through a breakup; you can have compassion for how painful the experience is because you've gone through it yourself. You can have compassion for their suffering and share a mutual understanding. This recognition emerges naturally as we develop as channels of light and experience the interconnected nature of consciousness.

Developing genuine compassion involves a delicate balance. We can open our hearts to feel what someone else is feeling without becoming overwhelmed by their pain or trying to rescue them from their necessary growth experiences. This balanced compassion requires both an open heart and clear boundaries—the ability to care deeply while recognizing that each soul has its journey and lessons to learn and integrate.

I remember a time when I started dating someone, only for my friends to warn me vehemently that this person was not right for me. I explained to them that I needed to explore this relationship so that I could learn about myself. My friends and I had a deep discussion about this, ultimately having compassion for my decision, but pulling back to protect themselves. This doesn't mean that they didn't care about me - quite the contrary, they cared for me enough to allow me to walk my path.

I've found that many spiritually sensitive people struggle with this balance. Some hide themselves from other people's pain, creating a false sense of spiritual detachment that blocks the heart's natural compassion. Others absorb other people's suffering so completely that they become depleted and unable to serve effectively. Balanced compassion allows us to feel with others while maintaining our center, to care deeply without becoming entangled in energy patterns that don't serve the highest good.

The development of balanced compassion often happens through challenging life experiences that break our hearts open while teaching us healthy boundaries. My journey of being sent to the monastery at thirteen, separated from my family, created both lasting pain and deep compassion. Through my suffering, I developed the capacity to be with others in their pain without needing to fix, rescue, or control their experience. I learned to offer presence rather than solutions, understanding rather than advice, and genuine care without expectation or attachment to outcomes.

As our spiritual awareness deepens, our compassion extends beyond human suffering to encompass all life forms and even the Earth itself. We begin to feel the pain of environmental destruction, the suffering of animals, and the discord in organizational and human systems as aspects of a unified field of consciousness to which we all belong. This expanded compassion naturally motivates us to make choices that reduce harm and increase well-being for the whole.

The great divide between spiritual knowledge and spiritual living is one I've witnessed in my own family. My father is an experienced numerologist and palm reader with extensive knowledge of psychic gifts, extraterrestrial phenomena, and metaphysical concepts. His intellectual understanding of these subjects is profound and inspiring. Yet, I've watched him struggle to integrate this spiritual knowledge into daily living.

Despite his deep understanding of spirituality, my father often falls into patterns of complaining, pessimism, and negativity in everyday life. This disconnect between spiritual awareness and emotional expression has created distance in our relationship, as it becomes difficult to maintain a connection with someone who struggles to receive kindness or express appreciation and often retorts with frustration. This experience has taught me that spiritual knowledge, no matter how extensive, serves little benefit without emotional integration, which allows us to embody those principles in our relationships and daily interactions. (Note: There is no shame or judgment toward my father; this is just my observation, and he is allowed to live in his truths, even if they don't align with mine.)

This pattern isn't unique to my father - many people on the spiritual path develop extensive knowledge of spirituality but continue to carry unhealed emotional wounds that affect their ability to live joyfully and appreciatively. True spiritual development isn't measured by what we know or what abilities we possess but by how we show up in our ordinary human interactions - our capacity for gratitude, kindness, and genuine presence with others.

The cultivation of compassion isn't separate from our spiritual practices, but it is integral to them. When we meditate, we can explicitly send loving kindness to other people's suffering. When we work with energy, we can set intentions for healing to benefit all beings, not just ourselves. When we connect with higher guidance, we can ask to be shown how to serve with greater compassion and effectiveness.

Another essential aspect of ethical living is authenticity - the willingness to be genuinely ourselves rather than conforming to external expectations or spiritual stereotypes. True authenticity requires tremendous courage, especially when our truest form of self-expression may challenge conventional norms or spiritual ideals.

Many people on a spiritual path fall into the trap of spiritual bypassing, using spiritual concepts or practices to avoid dealing with uncomfortable emotions, unresolved wounds, or challenging aspects of the human experience. They adopt a spiritual persona that presents as perpetually positive, peaceful, and transcendent while suppressing authentic feelings and needs that don't fit this idealized image.

Paradoxically, the attempt to appear 'spiritual' actually blocks the authentic flow of light through us. True channels of light aren't perfect - far from it. We are not people who are perpetually quiet and never experience doubt, fear, anger, or confusion. We are fully human individuals who dare to embrace and integrate all aspects of our humanity while remaining connected to higher dimensions of consciousness. We allow ourselves to experience the good, bad, and ugly without shame, guilt, or judgment.

I've seen how performative spirituality - trying to appear more evolved, peaceful, or transcendent than we genuinely feel - creates energetic distortions that block our channel. When we present a spiritual facade while suppressing our authentic emotions and experiences, we create an inner division that denies the natural flow of light. Authentic expression, even of our struggles and shadows, creates a clearer channel than spiritual pretense.

I do not aspire for perfection. I embrace all aspects of myself without dimming my light or suppressing my feelings of failure. I understand that every aspect of my existence is necessary for my path forward. Not long ago, I had a powerful lesson that changed how I view my work and purpose forever.

After investing five figures in a mentorship program with an intuitive coach to learn marketing techniques and receive energy healing, I felt proud of myself for being so immersed in a new way of communication and marketing for potential clients. But the moment our coaching relationship ended, I heard a very clear, loud voice from God telling me: "Congratulations on finishing your program. I would like for you to unlearn everything that you've learned, starting today."

Unlearn? Are you serious?

I was shocked and confused. Why would God ask me to unlearn what I had just spent so much money on to learn? It took me quite a few weeks to accept this request, but I gradually understood that God has His reasons, and who am I to judge or question them? The marketing techniques and approaches I had learned were connected to my mentor's energy and perspective. To become a proper channel of light, I needed to find my authentic voice and expression, rather than trying to model someone else's, no matter how successful they seemed to be.

Approximately a month later, I started rebuilding my business using my own energy and authentic expression, rather than adopting my mentor's templates and approaches. It took some practice to find my voice, but the results were remarkable - my business grew by leaps and bounds in ways that would never have been possible had I continued trying to channel someone else's light rather than my own. This experience taught me that authentic expression isn't just spiritually fulfilling but also practical and effective, even if we can't see the big picture. When we align with our own truth and unique gifts, just as God had requested of me, we become clearer channels for the specific light we're here to bring into the world.

But I want to emphasize - this was my guidance. Your path might be different. Sometimes we need external teachings, other times we need to trust our inner voice. The key is developing discernment about what's right for you.

This doesn't mean indulging every emotional reaction or speaking every thought with reckless abandon. Authenticity exists in balance with compassion and discernment. We can acknowledge our genuine feelings and experiences while choosing how to express them in ways that serve the highest good of all concerned. The key distinction is between making a conscious choice about expression versus suppressing or denying what's genuinely present.

When we bring our authentic selves forward, we create permission for others to be authentic as well. When we dare to share both our light and our struggles, we create spaces where others can bring their whole selves without fear of judgment. This authentic presence does more to elevate consciousness than any spiritual teaching delivered from behind a perfect facade.

As we develop spiritually, I want you to know that service is not mandatory or an obligation, but rather it becomes a natural expression of our expanding consciousness. We serve not because we should or because we're trying to earn spiritual badges, but because we recognize other people around us as extensions of ourselves. Service becomes the joyful overflow of the light we're channeling rather than something we do from a sense of duty or sacrifice. It doesn't mean that you will go around befriending your enemies, but rather that you understand that hurt people will hurt people.

The Buddhist teachings I learned as a child emphasized that genuine service arises from your authentic nature rather than obligation. I see 'service' as a way you exist and express yourself in every aspect of daily life. The Christian parable of the Good Samaritan teaches similar principles about service arising naturally from compassion rather than religious obligation.

If you are feeling defensive, it may be that pain is expressing itself louder than our most authentic and purest form because you are hurt and misunderstood. If you are angry, it may be that the world you've experienced is tainted with dark experiences that cloud your current reality. That is not your authentic nature. When we understand that our purest, authentic form is that of simplistic kindness, we recognize that the frustrations and hard emotions in our lives are a reflection of pain and suffering we've experienced.

When we understand that we are all connected and more alike than ever through the lens of compassion, helping ourselves becomes a priority, and caring for others becomes as natural as caring for our own body and nourishing it. 'Service' is not something we need to do to prove our spiritual worth, but a natural expression of our recognition that all beings are part of the same living system, including all of the emotions we can ever experience in life.

The desire to serve and help others manifests uniquely in each individual, shaped by their gifts, circumstances, and soul purpose. For example, the accountant who brings his A-Game, integrity, and diligence to financial dealings operates just as powerfully as an intuitive healer working in the realm of energy fields. A parent raising children with warmth and kindness serves as an influential spiritual teacher in the world. The key isn't about what we do, but how your purest consciousness flows through whatever path you are walking, whenever and wherever.

This aligns with the Christian teaching about spiritual gifts, where Paul explains that different gifts are given to different people, but all are valuable for the common good. The Buddhist concept of "right livelihood" similarly emphasizes that any work can be spiritual when done with the right intention.

True service or help invites reciprocity and mutual benefit, rather than one-way giving. One-way giving can often lead to depletion, and we don't want that to happen. When we help others from a place of authentic alignment with our gifts and purpose, we receive just as much as we give. This may feel uncomfortable at first because you've been taught to 'be good' and 'share', but the Laws of the Universe ask that you have a mutual exchange of energy. Energy flows through us, not directly from us, creating sustainable service that nourishes rather than depletes. This sustainability becomes increasingly important as our service expands, allowing us to contribute over the long term rather than burning brightly and then burning out.

It's important to understand that authentic service and help do not mean violating your boundaries for the sake of others. Quite the opposite is true. Genuine service involves a deep connection with yourself that allows you to honor your boundaries while offering your gifts. Without healthy boundaries, service quickly becomes depletion, resentment, and eventually burnout. The light you're here to channel becomes diminished when your well-being is compromised.

Many spiritual teachings have been misinterpreted to suggest that selflessness means removing your own needs, saying yes to every request, or making yourself constantly available to everyone but yourself. I was taught this when I was raised in a Buddhist monastery, which led me to fall into a deep pattern of people pleasing.

I do not believe that spirituality means that you need to be a pushover. I've seen too many light workers, healers, and spiritual practitioners sacrifice their health, relationships, and joy on the altar of service, believing this martyrdom was somehow noble or necessary. This approach diminishes the quality and sustainability of what they offer, while creating unhealthy dynamics with those they serve.

True boundaries aren't walls that disconnect you from others but clear energetic containers that allow you to serve from a place of wholeness rather than fragmentation. They define what's yours to carry and what belongs to others. They clarify where your responsibility begins and ends. They protect your energetic integrity so that what flows through you remains clear and uncorrupted.

Establishing and maintaining healthy boundaries requires ongoing inner understanding, empathy, and courage. You must be willing to check in with your inner feelings before saying yes to requests or opportunities. You need the clarity to recognize when serving in a particular way would compromise your well-being or integrity. And you need the courage to communicate your limits clearly and compassionately, even when others might be disappointed or put pressure on you.

I've found that those with the clearest boundaries often provide the most profound service because their offerings come from a place of fullness rather than depletion. They know when to say no so that their yes retains its power and integrity. They understand that temporary disappointment is preferable to the resentment that comes from overextending beyond true capacity.

I've seen people who try to serve others through sheer will and effort, pushing beyond their energetic capacity or authentic calling, often create dependency rather than empowerment. True service acknowledges the dignity and innate wholeness of those we serve. We offer our gifts not because others are broken and need fixing, but because we recognize their inherent divinity and want to support their awakening and flourishing.

We also recognize that service happens on multiple levels simultaneously. While our physical actions matter tremendously, we also serve through our energetic presence and the quality of consciousness we bring to every interaction. Sometimes our greatest service comes through simply being fully present with another person, holding space for their process without trying to change or fix their experience.

As our consciousness expands, we naturally feel a growing sense of responsibility for the well-being of the whole. We recognize that our choices—what we consume, how we speak, where we direct our resources, and how we treat others—create ripples that affect the entire web of life. This recognition can feel overwhelming at times, as we become increasingly aware of suffering, injustice, and environmental degradation happening globally.

Let's be real here - many people don't understand how powerful and influential they are. You are a channel of light, and it requires courage to be authentically you. Some people will retreat into spiritual bypassing, focusing exclusively on raising their vibration while avoiding engagement with challenging collective issues. Others may become overwhelmed by the scale of global problems, falling into despair or frantic activism driven more by fear than by grounded wisdom.

Living with universal responsibility as a channel of light requires finding the middle path between these extremes. We neither deny our interconnection with global challenges nor become overwhelmed by them. Instead, we bring presence, compassion, and discernment to determining how we're called to contribute within our sphere of influence.

The Buddhist concept of 'skillful means' (upaya) offers insightful guidance here. It teaches us that wisdom expresses itself through actions appropriate to specific circumstances and the needs of those involved by people who are skilled in that area. Similarly, the Christian concept of "gifts of the Spirit" suggests that each person has unique ways of serving.

Not everyone is called to address climate change, systemic injustice, or other collective challenges in the same way. Some will contribute through direct activism, others through conscious business practices, others by raising conscious children, and others through energy work that helps shift the collective consciousness. All of these paths are valid expressions of universal responsibility when followed with authentic expression, integrity, and genuine care.

What matters the most isn't how vast your contribution is in the world, but how we show up in the world itself. A small act done with clear intention and genuine compassion can have a more positive impact than grand, sweeping gestures performed from ego or obligation. As channels of light, we trust that when each person follows their authentic calling with integrity and compassion, the collective needs will be addressed through our complementary contributions.

This inner trust and honoring of your truth doesn't mean passivity or denial of urgent global challenges. It means you engage in actions guided by higher wisdom, rather than fear or external pressure. If you are feeling internal pressure, it means that something external to you is influencing the way you are showing up. It means that you will need to distill and discern what is yours to do and do it wholeheartedly, while trusting others to fulfill their unique roles in the larger world.

Perhaps the most profound way we exercise universal responsibility is through the quality of our authenticity we bring to every moment and interaction. I always tell my students and clients that what matters most is how you show up in the world around you. Are you hiding, retreating, afraid, or plain authentic? Every time we respond to a situation from a place of centeredness rather than being reactive, our energy ripples out into the world around us, affecting everyone we encounter and extending far beyond what we can see or understand. Your job is to simply show up and be the most authentic version of yourself everywhere you go.

Research on social contagion demonstrates that emotional states and behaviors spread through social networks like viruses, influencing people up to three degrees of separation from the original source. When you maintain a calm, compassionate, and authentic presence during a challenging situation, that quality of energy you embody doesn't just affect the person you're directly engaging with - it potentially influences dozens or even hundreds of others through subsequent interactions.

When we operate from a place of conscious awareness, we recognize that our primary responsibility is to maintain clear alignment with our higher connections, moment by moment, in the ordinary circumstances of our lives. This ongoing practice of conscious presence creates a field of coherence that helps others access their inner wisdom and compassion. We become walking 'permission slips' for others to embody more of their authentic light.

This understanding transforms how we see everyday interactions and choices. The way we respond to the stressed cashier, the honesty we bring to difficult conversations, the integrity we maintain when no one is watching - all of these become opportunities to channel light into the collective field. No moment is too small or mundane to serve as a vehicle for higher consciousness when we bring our full presence to it.

When we embrace our role in the collective awakening, we hold a both/and perspective on individual and collective transformation. We recognize that our awakening and larger systemic change are not separate processes but complementary aspects of a unified evolution of consciousness.

Spirituality without engagement with the world around you can become self-absorbed escapism. Activism without spiritual grounding often recreates the very dynamics it seeks to transform. The integration of inner work and outer service creates sustainable transformation at both individual and collective levels.

This integration involves bringing spiritual awareness to how we engage with social, economic, political, and environmental systems. Rather than dismissing these systems as "lower vibration" concerns irrelevant to spiritual development, we recognize them as crucial arenas for embodying higher consciousness. The choices we make as citizens, consumers, community members, and professionals all reflect our spiritual values and awareness.

At the same time, we avoid the trap of believing that systemic change alone will create a more conscious world without corresponding shifts in individual awareness. We recognize that transformed systems require transformed individuals to create and sustain them. Our personal spiritual development isn't separate from social transformation; it's an essential foundation for creating lasting, positive change.

Ethical living isn't about having all the perfect answers or following a rigid moral code. It's about living the questions with presence, humility, and genuine care. In a complex world with no easy solutions to many challenges, we commit to bringing our clearest awareness and deepest compassion to each choice we face. I wholeheartedly believe that this is the only way.

This means being willing to reexamine the assumptions we make, listening to perspectives different from our own, and adjusting our understanding as we receive new information and insights. It means approaching complex ethical questions with both principled conviction and humble openness to deeper understanding.

On this path of spiritual growth, we recognize that ethical living isn't about achieving moral perfection but about ongoing alignment with the highest truth we can access in each moment - the good, bad, the ugly. We forgive ourselves when we fall short, learn from our mistakes, and continually recommit to bringing more integrity, compassion, and consciousness to our lives and service.

As you continue developing your spiritual gifts, I invite you to reflect on how you're called to embody your light in service to the whole. Do you live from a place of trust or fear? Do you exist to people please or to honor your authenticity? These questions aren't about adding more obligations to your life or trying to save the world through sheer effort, but about understanding that your authenticity, your work, your energy, your perspective, and your choices influence a greater world around us. It's about listening deeply to where and how your unique gifts are needed, and allowing yourself to flow into that service and express it with joy and authenticity.

Remember that you're not alone in this journey. Millions of awakened souls are showing up and bringing their unique gifts to the collective transformation underway on our planet. When we each fulfill our part with integrity and compassion, the whole is served in ways more beautiful and effective than any single person could orchestrate.

The world doesn't need you to be perfect. It needs you to be authentic, to bring your whole self: light and shadow, strength and vulnerability, wisdom and not-knowing - to the great work of channeling higher consciousness into form. Your willingness to show up fully and align your life with the light you're channeling creates ripples of transformation far beyond what you can see or measure.

I want to emphasize that everything I've shared in this chapter comes from my journey and understanding. Your path to ethical living and universal responsibility may look entirely different, and that's not just okay - it's essential. Spiritual independence means taking what resonates from various teachers and traditions, including what I've shared, while always returning to your inner wisdom as the final authority.

Whether you resonate with Buddhist compassion, Christian love, indigenous wisdom, quantum consciousness, or your own direct experience, or some combination of all of these, what matters most is that you live from your authentic truth. The greatest gift you can give the world is your genuine self, expressing spirit in your unique way.

Those walking this path hold a vision of a world where every being can flourish, where systems support rather than suppress the full expression of human potential, where our relationship with Earth is one of reciprocity rather than exploitation. This vision isn't mere wishful thinking but a potential future we help create through our choices and presence each day.

In the quiet moments of alignment, in the courageous choices to speak the truth with compassion, in the small acts of kindness and the bold stands for what matters most - this is where we channel light into a world that deeply needs what each of us uniquely brings. This is how we live the universal responsibility that comes with awakening to our true nature as beings of light.

You do you, boo.

Chapter 13: Navigating Spiritual Challenges and Dark Nights of the Soul

(Note: I've shared some stories in this chapter that might be triggering. If you're sensitive, please consider skipping it for now.)

The spiritual journey isn't always sunshine and rainbows. For many of us, the path includes periods of profound darkness, doubt, and struggle that can shake us to our core. These challenging phases have been called many names across traditions - the dark night of the soul, spiritual emergency, the void, or simply the great awakening or unraveling. Whatever we call them, these difficult times are not signs of failure but necessary experiences of our spiritual evolution.

My own experiences with dark nights of the soul are something I would never wish upon my worst enemy.

I remember sitting on the steps of my home in Pasadena, California, having been retriggered into a state of abandonment and profound terror. The guy my friends had warned me not to date turned out to be a real disaster. They were right, but I had to experience it for myself.

Staring into a full moon with tears running down my face, I

blasted my frustrations at the Universe with questions like, "Why me? Why this? Why now?" The darkness above me offered no answers or solace that night. I cried myself to sleep - one of many teary nights. Only decades later did I recognize that specific, excruciating moment of pain I experienced was meant to train and guide me. Using these moments of suffering, I learned to use empathy for myself and later empathize with others navigating their darkness. Nothing theoretical can replace the wisdom and truth that comes from having walked through the fire yourself.

The term "dark night of the soul" originates from the writings of 16th-century mystic St. John of the Cross, who described a painful period of spiritual purification that comes before a deeper connection with the divine. What makes these periods particularly challenging is that they often happen while we're experiencing spiritual openings or awakenings. Just when we think we're making progress, the ground turns to quicksand and seems to disappear beneath our feet. The very practices and beliefs that once brought joy and comfort may suddenly feel empty or inaccessible.

Though painful, these dark nights are meant to guide us in our personal development. They strip away illusions, dissolve outdated identities, clear away spiritual inaccuracies, and prepare us for more authentic and grounded expressions of our truth. Without these challenging periods in our lives, our spiritual growth would remain superficial at best - just intellectual understanding without the depth of emotions that transform our entire being through difficulty. The most challenging moments in our lives are often seen as lessons so that we can access that next level.

Many spiritual traditions recognize this pattern of descent before ascent, of darkness before greater light. In Greek mythology, heroes like Persephone and Orpheus had to journey into the underworld before emerging with greater wisdom and power. Indigenous traditions worldwide incorporate ceremonial descents into darkness as initiation rites. The Buddha's enlightenment came only after periods of extreme temptation and after confronting Mara, the Lord of Death. Christ experienced his forty days in the wilderness and the agony in Gethsemane before his resurrection. These archetypal patterns remind us that spiritual growth often requires passage through the darkest territories of our being.

Beyond my profound spiritual crises, the Universe has allowed me to experience many horrifying breakups that have challenged me to rediscover my inner strength, courage, and resilience. I don't claim that any path to healing is easy. However, it's important to acknowledge that there is beauty in healing - unfortunately, it's difficult to see it when you're going through it. The perspective that transforms pain into wisdom usually comes later, when the acute suffering has subsided enough for us to recognize the growth that has occurred.

These difficult times tend to share common characteristics, regardless of whether they are triggered by external circumstances, such as loss and heartbreak, or arise seemingly from nowhere during periods of spiritual practice. Usually, there's a sense of disorientation and loss of meaning. Things that once felt joyful and certain now appear questionable. There may be intense emotional states - grief, fear, anger, or emptiness - that don't resolve through our usual coping mechanisms. Many people describe feeling abandoned by spiritual guidance or presence that had previously been reliable.

It's important to distinguish between clinical depression and the spiritual process of the dark night. While they may share some symptoms, their nature and purpose differ significantly. Depression typically involves a shutting down of energy and consciousness, while the dark night, though painful, often involves a deep intensification of awareness and sensitivity. Both deserve appropriate care, and they can certainly co-exist, but recognizing the spiritual dimension of our struggles can prevent unnecessary suffering.

Physical symptoms often accompany these spiritual challenges. Disrupted sleep, changes in appetite, unusual body sensations, or waves of energy moving through the body can all be part of the experience. Our nervous system registers spiritual crisis just as it does any other threat or major transition. Understanding this can help us respond with appropriate self-care rather than adding self-judgment to our struggles.

The dark night often brings forward powerful challenges to our identities and belief systems. Aspects of ourselves that seemed essential may suddenly feel hollow or untrue. Beliefs we've held onto with certainty may start to crumble under the intensity of the healing crisis. This dissolving and dismantling of our realities, while disorienting, makes space for more authentic and direct wisdom to emerge. We move from believing to knowing, from conceptual understanding to embodied wisdom through experience.

When I work with clients moving through these dark times, I remind them that the goal isn't to escape the darkness as quickly as possible, but rather to remember that nothing is permanent. You can develop the capacity to be present with what's arising, even if it's pain and suffering. The natural human tendency is to resist the heaviness, to try to think or spiritualize our way out of it. But the quickest way through is usually straight through the middle, with mindful awareness and self-compassion as our companions.

When going through periods of uncertainty, I've found it helpful to ask myself, "What is the lesson here?" This simple question reframes the experience from something happening to me to something happening for me. Even if I can't immediately see the purpose or blessing, approaching the difficulty with open curiosity to its potential gift changes my relationship to the pain.

Other good questions include:

What do I need the most right now?

What can I do to shift my perspective, situation, or path forward?

These questions invite us to explore the root cause of what's creating the suffering within us and what we need to develop as an antidote. Instead of spiraling into the experience of pain and being consumed by it, we dive deeper to discover its origins and meaning.

When an ex of mine was deployed to the Middle East during the height of the Iraq War, I remember feeling consumed by emotion and spiraling into chaos. Anytime I saw news related to the military, I would break down into tears. I felt like I had lost control of my central nervous system, which further caused me to panic. When I recognized what was happening, I stopped reading or watching the news. I stayed focused by reading happy books and started journaling about all the things that were bothering me. I kept asking myself why:

> Why am I feeling this way?
> Is it the end of the world?
> What is being triggered beneath the surface?
> Is it truly mine?
> What do I need to know?
> What do I need to do?

This process of inquiry helped me discover that my panic wasn't just about the long-distance relationship but connected to much earlier experiences of abandonment that had never been fully processed. Once I identified the origin of my panic, it became easier to navigate. Instead of blaming my partner for deploying, I was able to go deep into my own experiences and heal those original traumas. I had to first name the emotion I was feeling - in this case, abandonment. Then I could address it directly rather than being swept away by its current. Being a military girlfriend was one of the hardest things I've ever done in my life, outside of setting free the corporate identity I had created for myself to become a shaman. Again, I had to go through those tiered experiences to discover and uncover the most authentic version of myself.

This approach of identifying emotions, exploring their origins, and discerning their lessons provides a practical way through any spiritual challenge. When we name our experience and see it as lessons, we begin to develop some space around it. We're no longer completely identified with the pain but can hold it in awareness. From this slight bit of distance, we can then inquire more deeply into its roots and messages.

The process isn't linear, and we often cycle through phases of emotion multiple times before true integration occurs. During these cycles, please remember not to abandon or gaslight yourself by dismissing your feelings as unspiritual or unnecessary. Every emotion serves a purpose, carrying energy and information that contributes to your wholeness. Honor and respect the emotions that arise, giving them space to be fully experienced without judgment, of course, without hurting others in the process.

Many spiritual traditions offer wisdom for navigating these challenging territories. The Buddhist concept of equanimity—maintaining mental stability and composure in the face of life's fluctuations—provides a valuable perspective. Equanimity doesn't mean not feeling our emotions, but developing the capacity to be with them without being overwhelmed. Instead of becoming the emotions, you learn to observe them as a silent participant. This allows you to learn more about yourself without being swept away. It's about finding the middle path between suppressing and indulging our feelings.

The mystical branches of many religions speak directly to the experience of divine absence, also known as the "cloud of unknowing." These traditions remind us that feeling separated from the sacred may be a necessary phase in developing a more mature spiritual connection. Like a parent who gradually removes external support so a child can learn to walk independently, these periods of apparent absence may be invitations to develop a more internal, autonomous spiritual foundation.

Indigenous wisdom traditions often emphasize the importance of community support during spiritual initiation. While the individual must ultimately face their own darkness, they need not do so in isolation. Elders who have traversed similar territory can provide guidance, context, and reassurance that what seems like madness or failure is a recognized and honored phase of development.

Something I've seen in both my journey and when working with clients is that spiritual crises often coincide with significant energy shifts in the body. The kundalini awakening process, for instance, can trigger profound dark nights as energy moves through blocked areas of our system. What feels like depression or anxiety may be stuck energy beginning to move, attempting to clear old patterns and traumas stored in the body. Understanding this energetic dimension can help us approach spiritual challenges with greater awareness and insight. Sometimes the most helpful response isn't more thinking or analysis but gentle movement practices, sound healing, or energy work that supports the body's natural clearing process. The body holds its wisdom and timeline for healing that the rational mind can't always access or control.

I've found that when things become difficult, the usual meditation practices can sometimes intensify my stress rather than add a slice of calm. Instead of forcing meditation, I might try other activities like walking in nature, gardening, gentle yoga, or simply placing my hands on my heart while breathing deeply. These simple practices have helped me regulate my nervous system enough that I can be present with difficult emotions without becoming completely overwhelmed by them.

This points to an important principle for navigating dark nights: the practices that served us in other phases may not be what we need during deep spiritual challenges. We might need to temporarily set aside more expansive meditation techniques in favor of practices that help us feel safely held in our bodies and basic life routines. Later, as we stabilize, we can gradually reincorporate more spacious awareness practices. There is no one-size-fits-all approach.

The relationship between psychological healing and spiritual transformation becomes particularly important during dark nights. While traditional psychology may not fully understand the spiritual dimensions of crisis, its insights into trauma, attachment, and developmental processes offer valuable perspectives. Often, spiritual opening accelerates psychological healing by bringing previously unconscious material into awareness, where it can be integrated and processed.

In contrast, psychological healing creates a more stable container for spiritual expansion. When our emotional foundation is relatively secure, we can open to broader spiritual energies without becoming fragmented. This doesn't mean we must be perfectly healed psychologically before spiritual development can occur, but rather that these processes ideally unfold in dialogue with each other.

One of the more painful aspects of spiritual crisis can be the sense of isolation it creates. In a culture that celebrates independence, positivity, and quick fixes, those experiencing profound spiritual darkness often feel they must hide their struggles or risk rejection. Many spiritual communities inadvertently reinforce this isolation by subtly suggesting that spiritual positivity is the only way to heal. Sometimes, we just need to turn on a water faucet to let the mud out so that the water can eventually run clear.

The truth is that every great spiritual teacher and mystic throughout history has documented periods of tremendous struggle, doubt, and darkness. These passages aren't detours from the spiritual path but cover essential emotional, spiritual, mental, and physical territories on the journey to ancient wisdom. When we can acknowledge this reality, we create space for authentic sharing of spiritual challenges, reducing the isolation that compounds suffering. Nobody is ever immune to pain and suffering.

In the darkest times, a simple human connection can provide more healing than any spiritual technique. A friend who could sit with me without trying to fix or change my experience, who could hold space for my pain without judgment or fear, was worth more than a thousand spiritual platitudes. Sometimes the most spiritual thing we can offer each other is our wholehearted presence alongside them in their suffering.

This points to another aspect of navigating spiritual challenges - the need for appropriate support. Depending on the nature and intensity of what you're experiencing, this might include spiritual teachers or mentors who've navigated similar territories, therapists who understand spiritual experiences, energy workers, or simply friends who can remain steady while you move through instability.

In choosing support, discernment is essential. Not every friend, spiritual teacher, or therapist understands the territory of spiritual emergency or the dark night of the soul. Some may pathologize genuine spiritual processes, while others might spiritualize psychological issues that need direct attention. The most helpful guides are often those who can hold both perspectives - honoring the spiritual significance of your experience while also addressing practical needs for stability and integration.

The dark night often involves a raw confrontation with the mortality and limitations of an individual's existence. We face our deepest fears of annihilation and loss of control, discovering that we cannot protect ourselves from life's fundamental uncertainty. The surrender of any illusion of control often leads to a deeper trust in life itself and a more authentic relationship with the unknown.

I've developed a robust toolkit of resources for navigating spiritual challenges that I freely share with clients facing similar difficulties. While not every tool works for every person or situation, having multiple options increases our resilience when facing the unknown. Here are some approaches that many find helpful:

Developing a relationship with the darkness itself, approaching it with curiosity rather than fear or resistance.
What if this darkness has something to teach that light alone cannot reveal?
What treasures might be hidden in these shadows?
This shift in perspective can transform our experience alone.

You'll want to simplify your daily life during challenging times. Dark nights demand a great deal of energy for inner processing. Temporarily reducing commitments, simplifying decisions, and creating extra space for rest can provide the resources needed for this deep inner work.

You may want to get yourself into nature to breathe in fresh air and allow your heightened emotions to settle. Natural settings remind us that darkness and light, death and rebirth, are natural cycles of life. Witnessing these rhythms in the natural world can normalize our own experience of moving through difficulty toward renewal.

Perhaps you go back to old hobbies - activities, or hobbies often create an outlet for energies and emotions that cannot be easily articulated. Writing, dance, movement, sound, creative arts - any artistic form can help release and integrate what might otherwise remain stuck in our systems.

Have you considered finding the right balance of community and solitude? While connection and friendship help us feel less alone, there is also merit in having sufficient personal space for introspection and integration. Learning when to seek support and when to turn inward is part of developing spiritual discernment.

Ritual and ceremony can provide powerful containers for moving energy past spiritual limitations. Many traditions offer rituals specifically designed for transitions, helping us consciously mark and honor these passages rather than simply enduring them. Creating your rituals can be powerful when they hold space for you to authentically express your experience and intention.

Dreamwork can also be a great way to process dark nights of the soul, using dreams to uncover hidden nuggets of wisdom and identify what needs to be healed. Instead of focusing on what happened in the dream, think about how you felt. What can you learn from that experience? Paying attention to dream symbols, recurring themes, and emotional responses can offer clues to what's happening beneath your conscious awareness.

Perhaps most importantly, and this deserves a proper mention, is holding ourselves with such radical compassion, patience, and love throughout the process. The tendency to judge ourselves for struggling - to see any challenge as evidence of failure - creates unnecessary suffering on top of the existing difficulty. Self-compassion doesn't mean indulging and sitting with every reaction, but extending the same care to ourselves that we would offer a good friend going through similar challenges.

Resilience, spiritual or not, isn't about avoiding difficulty but developing the internal resources to move through life's challenges without being defined or diminished by them. This resilience grows through practice, not theory. Every time we encounter a difficult chapter with consciousness and care, we develop greater capacity for future challenges.

My resilience has been forged through multiple dark nights, each one stripping away another layer of who I thought I was, revealing something more potent beneath. While I wouldn't have chosen these painful times, I recognize now how each one expanded my capacity to serve others, navigating similar territory. Nothing builds credibility and compassion like having walked the path yourself.
Faith also evolves through these challenging passages. The blind faith we might hold before facing any crisis is quite different from the faith that emerges from having questioned everything and still finding something true at our core. Post-dark night faith tends to be more nuanced, more tolerant of paradox and uncertainty, less attached to specific forms or beliefs, and more rooted in direct experience than external authority.

This transformed faith becomes an anchor during future storms. Having discovered that something powerful in us survives even the most severe stripping away of our core identity and belief, we develop trust in our capacity to handle whatever comes next. This doesn't mean future challenges won't be painful, but that we carry a deep knowing that we can and will survive and heal through whatever we experience.
What emerges through the dark night is a more integrated version of yourself - one that embraces the full spectrum of human experience rather than attempting to transcend or bypass our humanity. We develop the capacity to hold light and shadow, joy and sorrow, knowing and mystery as complementary rather than opposing forces. This integration allows us to be more authentically present with the full complexity of life, both our own and others'.

The spiritual maturity gained through navigating dark nights enables us to hold greater complexity and paradox. We become less rigid in our beliefs, more comfortable with not-knowing, and more able to respond to life's challenges with creative adaptability rather than fixed formulas. This flexibility doesn't mean abandoning our values or spiritual foundations, but rather holding them in a more spacious, evolving relationship.

Over time, we may even develop a paradoxical sense of gratitude for the dark nights that have shaped us to who we are today. Not because suffering itself is desirable, but because of how these deep waves of life have deepened our humanity, expanded our compassion, and connected us to dimensions of experience we might never have discovered through comfort alone.

I certainly wouldn't have chosen the painful spiritual crises and heartbreaks that have punctuated my journey. Yet I can honestly say that I wouldn't be capable of the depth of presence and understanding I bring to my work without having navigated these territories personally. The light I channel now shines more clearly, precisely because it has been refined through darkness.

If you're currently moving through your own dark night, please know that you're not alone, you're not failing, and this period, however excruciating it feels right now, will not last forever. The darkness has its purpose in the greater unfolding of your wisdom. Trust the process even when you cannot see where it's leading. Reach for support when you need it, rest when you need to, and remember that dawn eventually follows even the longest night.

When you emerge from this chapter - and you will emerge - you'll carry a light that could only have been kindled in darkness, a wisdom that no book or teacher could have given you, and a capacity to be with others in their suffering that represents one of the greatest gifts any human can offer another. Your dark night isn't a failure, it's a necessary initiation into a deeper, more authentic embodiment of your light, your most powerful channel of light.

Chapter 14: Establishing Healthy Boundaries in Spiritual Practice

When you become a channel of light, establishing and maintaining healthy boundaries becomes not just important but essential for maintaining your brightness. Many people mistakenly believe that spiritual development means dissolving and merging all boundaries with others. This is not the case, and it's not about being completely open and available to everyone and everything. This misconception has led so many sensitive people into states of energetic depletion, confusion, and even spiritual crisis.

The truth is: the more spiritually open you become, the more important it is to have clear boundaries.

Boundaries in spiritual practice aren't walls that separate you from others but conscious containers that allow you to serve from a place of wholeness rather than fragmentation. Your boundaries define what energies you allow into your field, how you share your gifts with others, and how you protect your well-being while remaining open to genuine connection. Without these boundaries, your light can quickly become dimmed or distorted by influences that don't serve your highest good or the good of those you're here to help.

I learned this lesson the hard way during my years in the corporate world. While working for a particular Fortune 100 company, I allowed my professional identity to completely overshadow every other aspect of my being. I was willing to work long hours and make sacrifices for the sake of our team - staying late, working weekends, taking on additional responsibilities beyond my job description, and even taking a pay cut. There was a certain pride in this commitment, almost altruistic, that came from being needed and valued in this high-status environment.

What I didn't realize was how this single-pointed focus was gnawing away at my true nature. I was 'giving' for all the wrong reasons. I was in denial about my spiritual gifts during this period, pushing them aside to fit into the corporate mold of professional expectations. There was no room for spirituality to exist in me. The more I poured myself into this narrow identity, the less I recognized myself when I looked in the mirror.

It's a slippery slope from there, working on something that seems meaningful, but the question I eventually had to face was: Is it really meaningful? Am I changing lives? Does this work truly align with who I am at a soul level?

Years later, after much inner work and intuitive listening, I felt an unmistakable urge telling me it was time to go. And I did. God wanted me to work in a different industry and take on a whole different line of work. I thought He was wrong and ignored it. But I started to repeat the same patterns over and over again. Eventually, because I am stubborn, I learned the lesson of honoring my energies and acknowledging all of my spirit guides, spirits, ancestors, and ghosts who were guiding or taunting me.

I started pursuing jobs that allowed for a better work-life balance, creating space to explore other dimensions of my life. This eventually led me to start a 501(c)(3) non-profit animal rescue in Los Feliz, California, complete with a board of directors and a facility, all while working a full-time job. Yet even then, I was still discovering who I was beneath the layers of professional identity.

This experience raises great questions that a lot of people face on the spiritual path:
- When you identify yourself primarily with your job or role, are you being your authentic self?
- Or are you still in the process of discovery?
- What price are you willing to pay to reveal your true nature?

These questions point directly to the importance of boundaries around your authentic identity - being conscious about what aspects of yourself you allow to be defined by external roles versus what remains sacred and internally defined.

Energetic boundaries are perhaps the most fundamental yet least understood aspect of spiritual development. The more sensitive you become to subtle energies, which naturally happens when you open as a channel of light, the more susceptible you become to the energetic states of others. Without proper protection, you can easily absorb others' emotions, thought patterns, and even physical symptoms, mistaking them for your own.

Not all spiritual people operate at high vibrational frequencies. This is an important truth, one of many, that spiritual seekers are not prepared for when they begin to open to non-physical dimensions. Just as humans exist along a spectrum of consciousness and intention, so do beings in other realms. It's important to discern which beings are connecting with you for your highest good versus those with their agendas that may not align with your well-being or purpose.

I often explain to my clients that spiritual guidance exists across four distinct categories, arranged in a framework from the highest to the most immediate levels. I mentioned them in Chapter 5 of this book, but they're worth repeating.

The first and highest level is the creator consciousness itself: God, Source, the Infinite Mind that designed and pervades all of existence. This is like the CEO of the Universe, the ultimate intelligence from which all beings and dimensions emerge.

Below the first is the second level, which consists of ascended masters and archangels – highly evolved beings who have either completed many cycles of physical incarnation or were created to administer universal energies. These beings operate primarily from non-physical dimensions but can project their consciousness into our realm when needed. They serve as teachers, protectors, and wayshowers for humanity's collective evolution.

The third level down includes our personal spirit guides and ancestral helpers – beings who have a more direct connection to our individual soul journey. Spirit guides may be souls we've known in past incarnations who now assist us from the non-physical realms. Ancestral helpers are family members who have passed on but maintain a loving connection with their descendants, offering protection and guidance.

The fourth level – which is where many begin their exploration of the unseen – consists of environmental energies, personal energy fields (auras), earthbound spirits, and energetic remnants or imprints. This category is closest to our physical experience and, therefore, is often the easiest to perceive, but it also contains the most confusion and potential for misinterpretation.

My strong recommendation is to work exclusively with the upper two levels to stay aligned with the highest frequencies. If you're unfamiliar with energy work, it makes little sense to work with the lower two levels because those spirits and energies can inadvertently lead you down misleading or depleting paths.

I only take directions from the highest source - what I call God or Universal Intelligence. This boundary around the energetic influences I allow to guide me has protected me countless times from confusion and energetic manipulation.

Negative influences come in many forms - not just from disembodied entities but from living people, environments, situations, and opportunities that don't align with your highest path. People who consistently drain your energy, physical spaces with heavy or discordant energy, media that promote fear or negativity, and even seemingly attractive opportunities that would take you away from your true purpose

- all these require clear boundaries to navigate wisely.

When it comes to entities, ghosts, or poltergeists, I approach them with the understanding that they are people without bodies. They deserve compassion but not reverence, and they certainly shouldn't be allowed to interfere with your well-being or that of your loved ones. If such presences are in your home or affecting your clients, you must establish firm boundaries around what you will and won't tolerate.

I remember a time when I was excited to go to a music concert. I rarely go to them because spirits have been known to follow me home, but since it had been a few years, I decided to go to the Mayan in Los Angeles to see an '80s tribute band. When we arrived at the venue, I was exhilarated that none of the spirits were bothering me. Score! When the concert finished, I was still surprised that nobody (spirits) was begging for my help. Once I got home, I removed my makeup and climbed into bed. I fell asleep a happy camper - until I was woken up at 1 am by a male spirit in his thirties, wearing a plaid red and blue button-up shirt and jeans, sitting in the armchair located at the foot of my bed. I immediately rolled my eyes and told him he could not be there. This spirit, not realizing it was 1 am, spent the next 5 minutes arguing that I could see him.

"You can see me, right?" he'd excitedly say.

"Yes, I can see you. But that's beside the point. You can't be here."

"But you can see me, right?"

"Yes, now is not a good time. It's 1 am, bro."

"But you can see ME?!!!"

"Listen, it's really late. This isn't appropriate, and you've entered my home without my permission. You need to get out now."

"But you can see me!! Nobody has ever SEEN ME!!"

I gave it another few minutes before pushing his energy beyond the walls of my house, and went back to bed 15 minutes later.

I've performed numerous exorcisms over Zoom for clients dealing with unwanted entities. The most important key is not to allow fear to overrule you. Once you're able to see a spirit for who or what they are, you must have such strong boundaries that you can confidently direct them out and back to Source. Just like dealing with pushy people, you want to use the same persistence and boundaries with spirits. No still means no, dead or alive.

I can work with spirits to help them cross over using the power of clear intention and a focused mind. My 1600 BC shamanic self had trained me to use my clairvoyant abilities to see and quickly channel the appropriate next steps. But the foundation is always to keep unwavering boundaries and alignment with the highest and purest light available.

A more recent personal experience taught me the importance of these boundaries with spirits. I once dated someone who I intuitively knew was composed of 50% darkness and 50% light - his soul was at a crucial decision point. When I shared this revelation with him, he was worried that his darkness would affect my light. I assured him this wouldn't happen because I was firmly established as a channel of pure light. During our relationship, God asked me to tell him that he stood at a critical juncture where he would need to choose either aspect of himself as the primary version going forward. He understood my message, but, ultimately, because everyone has their own free will, he began drifting toward darker pathways, eventually leading to our breakup and demise.

Some time after our separation, while I was reading a book, a spirit suddenly appeared in my psychic vision. I immediately recognized this woman as his mother, who had passed away years before - a woman with short white hair, neatly parted to the side, facing three-quarters away and looking into the distance. Though I had never met her in life, she recognized my ability to perceive her energy based on her connection to him. She had come to plead for my help.

I calmly explained to her that I don't work for spirits but only for God. When she persisted, pushing against my boundaries, I set a clear condition: if she could somehow prove the necessity of her request through some kind of spiritual sign, I would consider helping.

This is a true story. The very next day, while I was out to dinner with a few girlfriends, I received a text message from an unknown number that correctly spelled my name, "Sonya." It said,

"Sonya - would you and your son like to have a pool day at my house tomorrow?"

If you know me, you'll know that I don't have any children. My boys and girls have four legs, and there's no way they'd want a pool date.

Confused and concerned about who might be contacting me, I scoured through old text messages and even turned on my old backup computer to look into it. I couldn't find any instance of this phone number and had no idea who might think I have a son.

While looking through old text messages, I gravitated toward some old messages between my ex-boyfriend and me. I started going down memory lane, reminiscing about the old times when we were much happier. He had also sent me about 35 memes that I thought were quite funny. While scrolling through those photos, I came across something startling - wedged between the 30-some odd photos, a picture of a woman with short white hair, neatly parted to one side, facing three-quarters away and looking into the distance while standing on a boat, appeared on my screen.

I immediately recognized this as the sign his mother had orchestrated. I was both shocked and impressed. Speaking out to thin air, I exclaimed, "Bravo, lady. Bravo."

Based on this extraordinary confirmation, I made a single exception to check on my ex, but otherwise maintained my firm boundaries about which spiritual influences I respond to. No still means no, dead or alive.

This experience reinforced my understanding that while ancestors and other spirits may offer spiritual guidance and support, it is wise to trust only the path that God or Source reveals.

My ancestors, who continue to support and love me from behind the scenes, understand not to interfere with my life but rather to serve as invisible cheerleaders from beyond the veil. This boundary around how I receive spiritual guidance has kept me clear and protected throughout my development.

Emotional boundaries are equally valuable in any spiritual practice. Being of service does not mean bending over backward to help everyone at the expense of your energy, time, and happiness. This misconception has led so many lightworkers to places of depletion and burnout, ultimately diminishing their capacity to serve effectively.

True service flows from fullness, not from sacrifice that leaves you empty.

This is a painful story to tell, but worth sharing to illustrate a point. Following yet another devastating breakup where my partner left our shared home without explanation, following a second miscarriage, I fell into a deep depression. My abandonment issues had triggered a dark night of the soul.

Struggling with isolation and despair, I felt completely alone and lost. I was overwhelmed by shame, failure, and self-disgust.

In a fit of desperation, I called my uncle Clive (real name) for advice. This was a massive mistake because I should have known that Clive was emotionally unavailable and mentally unstable.

He answered the phone, not to soothe or calm my nerves, but instead cruelly told me that I was "dumb and stupid" and should kill myself.

"You're worthless. You're pathetic. You have nothing going on in your life. No wonder you're like this. Maybe you should just kill yourself. This world doesn't need you."

Honestly, I was beyond lower than low. His toxic words penetrated my weakened emotional boundaries, and I seriously pondered his horrible advice. Maybe he was right? Maybe I am useless and pathetic? Believing his words is a mistake that I will never forget. I tried to do what he told me to do. Yes, I did. I have no shame in admitting this fact because it pushed me to where I am today.

My best friend Janelle had seen my alarming posts on Facebook and immediately called the police for a wellness check. The police and fire department came and grabbed me from my demise. Not only was I embarrassed and humbled, but I was also admitted to the hospital and then to a mental health facility. By the time I had regained some clarity, even the facility's receptionist looked me up and down and said,

"Hmm, mmm, what have you done? You don't belong here,"

adding unnecessary judgment to an already painful situation.

The only thing I managed to take with me was Michael Newton's "Journey of Souls: Case Studies of Life Between Lives." This book was a saving grace that allowed me a modicum of sanity. It offered a perspective that shook me to my core, helping me understand that I had been pushed to my very edge precisely so I could realize and remember my true path. God hadn't forsaken me - I had been too stubborn to see the guidance that was always present. I read the entire book in the 72 hours I was placed on hold. I recall sharing a room with another girl who had tempted her fate and those who couldn't control themselves. On my way out, I met a man who had just been admitted for the same reason. I gave him the very same book and wished him luck.

This experience taught me the importance of emotional boundaries - being selective about whose opinions and energy I allow to affect me, especially during vulnerable periods. Had I had stronger emotional boundaries in place, I would have recognized my uncle's toxic words and immediately protected myself from their impact. I would have sought support from those who could hold space for my pain without judgment or harmful advice. I share this deeply personal story not to dwell on past trauma or relive certain pain, but to illustrate how emotional boundaries are crucial for our well-being and spiritual development. I am no longer in contact with my entire immediate and extended family for this reason - none of them, including my parents, supported me during my recovery.

Mental boundaries involve consciously choosing what thought patterns, belief systems, and information sources you allow to influence your mind. In today's world of constant information overload, establishing clear mental boundaries has become more essential than ever. This means being selective about what media you consume, through which devices, what teachings you integrate, and even which thoughts you choose to engage with versus those you simply observe and let go. Everything about life becomes an active meditation to identify and heal what does or does not serve you.

Many spiritual seekers naively absorb teachings from sources without actual discernment, buying into ideas that may not even be true. This is why I always encourage people to feel into what feels right to them. While being open to different perspectives has value, indiscriminately consuming information without contemplation creates a scattered energy field and unclear channel.

Mental boundaries include taking time to properly digest, absorb, and integrate information or teachings before moving to the next level, being willing to say "this isn't for me" to approaches that don't resonate with your truth, and maintaining your direct connection to guidance rather than becoming dependent on external authorities. When I mentor my clients, I teach them how to discern and feel the vibrations and energies, so they can understand what is meaningful and what isn't.

Physical boundaries include honoring your body's needs and limitations. Despite the common myth that transcending human physical needs represents a higher development, our bodies are not robots and require ongoing care to maintain good health. Ignoring your physical needs through excessive fasting, sleep deprivation, or pushing beyond genuine physical limitations does not accelerate your spiritual growth - it often creates an imbalance that requires later, deeper healing, because we need to unravel the effects of what was done.

During intensive spiritual work, your body may require more rest, specific nutrition, or particular environmental conditions to maintain clear balance. Honoring these needs doesn't make you any less spiritual, but actually honors and acknowledges the body's role in your work as a channel of light. Physical boundaries also include being conscious about who you allow into your personal space, how you arrange your environment to support your energy, and when you need solitude versus connection.

Temporal boundaries - those related to your time and availability - become increasingly important as your gifts develop and more people seek your assistance. Without clear boundaries around when and how you're available to others, you risk losing your energy, which reduces your effectiveness as a channel.

Please don't take this to mean that you need to be rigid or unavailable to anyone different from you, but rather to create sustainable containers of time and space that allow you to serve consistently over time, rather than in unsustainable bursts followed by burnout.

Now let's explore specific techniques for maintaining these various boundaries, beginning with energy protection practices:

The White Light Bubble is perhaps the easiest energy protection technique. Before beginning any spiritual work or entering challenging environments, visualize a sphere of brilliant white or golden light surrounding your body, extending about arm's length in all directions. Set the intention that this light allows only energies aligned with your highest good to enter while filtering out discordant or depleting influences.

Some practitioners enhance this basic technique by visualizing specific qualities in their protective field - crystal clarity for truth discernment, rose gold for heart protection, or electric blue for psychic defense.

Calling in Spiritual Protection from higher beings before energy work, channeling, or healing sessions creates an additional layer of boundary maintenance. This might involve invoking archangels, spiritual guides, or divine presence directly. The key is establishing a clear relationship with these higher forces and consistently acknowledging their supportive presence rather than making occasional desperate pleas when problems arise.

Regular energy clearing practices maintain healthy boundaries by preventing the accumulation of energetic residue from others. Just as you shower to cleanse your physical body, your energy field requires similar maintenance. Methods include visualization techniques where you see light washing through your field, sound clearing using bells or singing bowls, elemental clearing with smoke (such as sage or palo santo), salt baths, or movement practices that help release stuck energy.

Cord-cutting is another essential boundary maintenance practice that addresses energetic connections formed between you and others.

These energetic ties can persist long after the interactions have ended, continuing to drain your energy, sabotage, or transmit undesirable emotional states. Regular cord-cutting - visualizing or intending the release of these connections while maintaining only appropriate heart links - preserves energetic integrity.

I remember one distinct client session with a man who had come to me because he was tired of being jerked around by his ex-wife's abuse. Not only was he beaten to a pulp, but she also continued to manipulate his energy in his subconscious and sleeping states. When I remote viewed into his energetic body, via Zoom, I could see on his back that there were several cords, but also long shards of glass stabbed into his back. In addition to these long shards were smaller pieces of metaphysical glass designed to cause him harm.

I asked him to close his eyes as I began the healing experience. Using my clairvoyant eyes, I measured each piece of glass and slowly pulled them out one by one. I realize this sounds completely fanatical, but the man across the screen began to writhe and scream in pain. He sobbed hysterically with each movement until I was finished. Psychic work, as I know it, has very few limitations.

After I spoke to him, he felt lighter and freer. Although I haven't kept in touch with him, I've learned that he was able to start his own business and regain his health.

Having healthy boundaries doesn't mean you have to go to great lengths to sever loving connections, but rather to ensure they exist in balanced, life-supporting forms rather than as draining attachments.

Mindfulness of energetic exchanges helps maintain boundaries in the present moment. By developing an awareness of how different interactions, environments, and activities affect your energy, you can make conscious choices about how to engage. This might mean limiting time in certain environments, adjusting your energy before difficult interactions, or scheduling restoration time after particularly demanding exchanges.

Calling back your energy is a powerful way to reinforce your boundaries. Many sensitive people unconsciously project their energy outward - toward people they're concerned about, situations they're trying to control, or past events they're still processing. Regularly setting the intention to call back energy that's scattered in these ways restores your wholeness and reinforces natural boundaries.

Now let's consider a comprehensive list of spiritual practices that support healthy boundaries when approached with discernment:

Meditation creates internal space to recognize what's genuinely yours versus what you've absorbed from others. Regular meditation strengthens your connection to your center, making boundary discernment more natural.

Energy healing modalities like Reiki, Pranic Healing, or Quantum Healing provide frameworks for understanding energy dynamics, but they should be practiced with clear protection protocols.

Channeling higher wisdom can guide appropriate boundaries, but should be approached with careful discernment about which sources you're connecting with.

Divination practices, such as tarot, astrology, or the I Ching, offer a perspective on boundary challenges when used as tools for accessing your inner knowing, rather than as external authorities.
Breathwork can strengthen energetic boundaries by enhancing vital energy and clearing stagnant patterns that make boundaries permeable.

Movement practices like yoga, qigong, or conscious dance help integrate boundary awareness throughout your physical and energetic bodies.

Sound healing through chanting, toning, or instrumental sound helps reorganize your energy field and strengthen its coherence, enhancing natural boundaries.

Ceremony and ritual create designated containers for spiritual work, establishing clear boundaries between ordinary and sacred space and time.

Dream work provides insights into subconscious boundary patterns and often reveals where energy leaks or unhealthy connections exist.
Nature connection practices ground spiritual development in the wisdom of natural boundaries observed in ecosystems and natural cycles.

Journaling helps clarify internal boundaries between different aspects of self and illuminates where external boundary adjustments may be needed.

Shadow work reveals unconscious boundary patterns and helps integrate aspects of self that may be operating outside conscious awareness.

While all these practices offer potential benefits, they must be approached with discernment and clear boundaries. As I've mentioned, feel into what feels right to you. Any practice can become depleting or confusing when undertaken with imbalanced energy, inappropriate guidance, or without proper protection.

The ultimate foundation for healthy spiritual boundaries is a clear connection to your inner guidance system. When you're consistently attuned to your authentic truth, you naturally sense when something feels aligned versus when it creates discord, even if you can't immediately articulate why.

Developing trust in this inner compass requires practice and validation through experience, but it becomes your most reliable guide to boundaries over time.
I have met many people who confuse open-heartedness with a lack of boundaries. They feel obligated to help everyone who asks, to take on others' pain, to be available at all hours, or to freely share their gifts

without appropriate exchange. This pattern stems from misunderstanding the nature of accurate service and often leads to resentment, illness, and eventually withdrawal from service altogether. In my own experience, people also confuse my kindness with naivety. I am not naive, I simply choose to respond to the world in a way that enhances it, not detracts from it.

True compassion includes yourself in its consideration and embrace. It recognizes that maintaining your well-being is not an act of selfishness but is required for sustainable service. It understands that appropriate boundaries create the container that allows your gifts to flow rather than becoming diluted or distorted. It acknowledges that sometimes the most compassionate response is "no," making space for others to develop their tools and resources rather than becoming dependent on yours.

I've met people who have spirits attached to them that siphon their energy, both consciously and unconsciously. When I encounter such people, I always trust my intuition about how much time to spend with them and what energetic protection to maintain during interactions. This doesn't mean rejecting or judging them, but being realistic about the current energetic dynamic and my capacity to engage without depleting myself.

Developing discernment about which spiritual practices, teachers, and communities truly serve your highest development is another crucial aspect of boundaries. Not every path or teacher is appropriate for every seeker, and what serves you at one stage of development may become limiting at another. True spiritual discernment involves regularly checking in with yourself and feeling aligned with your evolving truth, while having the courage to make changes when needed.

Financial boundaries in spiritual work often challenge practitioners who feel uncomfortable charging for spiritual gifts or services. The belief that spiritual work should always be free creates an unsustainable model that often leads to depletion and resentment. An appropriate exchange - whether financial or through other forms of reciprocity - creates a healthy energy flow and acknowledges the value of what's being offered. This doesn't mean exploiting spiritual seekers, but instead establishing a clear and fair exchange that honors both the giver and the receiver.

Recognizing the warning signs of boundary violations helps you address imbalances before they become significant problems. These signs might include persistent fatigue after certain interactions, feeling confused about your feelings versus others', experiencing resentment about giving, having anxiety about saying no, or losing yourself in others' needs and expectations. When these signs appear, they're calling for boundary reassessment and adjustment rather than pushing through or ignoring the signals.

Maintaining healthy boundaries doesn't mean becoming rigid, closed, or defensive. True boundaries are flexible, responsive to changing circumstances, and permeable in appropriate ways. They allow authentic connection while preventing energy drain or confusion. They create safety that allows greater openness rather than walls that prevent relationships. They're expressed with calm clarity rather than defensive reactivity.

The paradox of spiritual boundaries is that clear boundaries allow for more genuine connection rather than less. When you're secure in your energetic integrity, you can open your heart more fully without fear of losing yourself in others. When you trust your discernment about which energies to allow into your field, you can explore expanded states of consciousness without confusion or depletion. When you honor your physical and temporal limitations, you create sustainable service that benefits more people over time.

I bear repeating myself, but the spiritual path will continually refine and evolve your understanding of appropriate boundaries. What served you at the beginning may need adjustment as your sensitivity and responsibilities grow. The key is maintaining ongoing awareness of how different energies, relationships, and practices affect your well-being and clarity, and making conscious adjustments as needed.

By establishing and maintaining healthy boundaries in all dimensions of your spiritual practice, you create the conditions for your light to shine with maximum clarity and impact. These boundaries aren't limitations on your spiritual potential but the very container that allows that potential to manifest in its fullest, most sustainable form.

Remember that, as a channel of light, your primary responsibility is to maintain the clarity and integrity of your channel. This requires honoring your needs, limitations, and trusting your intuition about what is appropriate. From this foundation of wholeness and clear containment, your light can flow in ways that truly serve without depleting your essential being. This is the art of setting spiritual boundaries - creating a sacred vessel through which universal light can flow with maximum clarity and minimal distortion.

Please protect your deepest truths.
Nobody else will do it for you until you do.

Chapter 15: Becoming a Channel of Light Here on Earth

As I sit here writing these final words to you, I am filled with a profound sense of gratitude and purpose. My entire life journey - through all the challenges, awakenings, and transformations we've explored in this book - has led me to this simple truth: my mission in this world is to light up as many other channels of light as possible. Each experience, each lesson, each moment of both darkness and illumination has brought me to this understanding.

I am here to fully embrace my light so that I can help ignite yours, creating a beautiful ripple effect as you, in turn, become your brilliant channel, guiding and lighting others onward and forward.

This isn't just a book to me. It's a heart-to-heart conversation between kindred souls. The words you're reading now flow directly from my soul to yours, carrying the energy and intention of awakening what already exists within you. Because we are all, at our essence, channels of light temporarily clothed in human form, here to remember our true nature and express it in our unique way.

I believe with every fiber of my being that we live in a time of unprecedented opportunity for spiritual awakening. Yes, we face enormous challenges as a global family - environmental crises, social injustice, political division, and the deep spiritual hunger that manifests as various forms of suffering. But alongside these challenges, an extraordinary wave of consciousness is expanding across our planet. More people than ever before are awakening to their spiritual nature, seeking deeper meaning, and feeling called to become vehicles for something greater than personal achievement or material success.

You picked up this book because something inside you resonated with the phrase "channel of light." Perhaps you didn't even know why it called to you, but some part of you recognized a truth your conscious mind might not fully comprehend yet.

Trust that inner knowing. It's your soul speaking to you about your true nature and purpose.

Throughout my journey from corporate executive to spiritual guide, from dark nights of despair to profound cosmic connection, I've learned that we don't need to seek light outside ourselves. We are that light, though it's often dimmed by layers of conditioning, fear, and forgetting. My purpose - my joy - is helping you remember this essential truth about yourself and providing practical pathways for letting your light shine more brightly and clearly in every aspect of your life.

This final chapter brings together everything we've explored, not as concepts to memorize but as living wisdom to embody. Being a channel of light isn't about achieving some rarified spiritual state accessible only to a chosen few. It's about recognizing and expressing your true nature, which is already connected to the vast field of universal consciousness and love that some call God, Source, or Divine Intelligence.

I use the term' channel" because it beautifully captures what happens when we align ourselves with a higher consciousness. A channel is a pathway through which something flows from one place to another. When you become a channel of light, you allow higher frequencies of wisdom, healing, and love to flow through you into this physical dimension, where they are so deeply needed.

You become the bridge between the seen and unseen realms, between potential and manifestation.

Light itself serves as both a literal phenomenon and a perfect metaphor for what we're discussing. Light illuminates, reveals truth, dispels darkness, nurtures life, and travels at the highest speed known in our Universe. When we speak of channeling light, we're talking about allowing these same qualities—clarity, truth, healing, vitality, and elevated consciousness—to flow through us into the world.

My path to becoming a channel of light wasn't straightforward. As I've shared throughout these pages, it included profound challenges - corporate burnout when I lost my identity in external achievement, heartbreaking loss that brought me to the edge of wanting to leave this world, encounters with darker energies that taught me discernment, and the ongoing practice of maintaining healthy boundaries while remaining open-hearted.

I share these experiences not to focus on the struggle but to remind you that whatever challenges you're facing aren't obstacles to your light - they're the very conditions that help your light grow stronger and clearer.

The Universe doesn't punish us, though it may sometimes feel that way when we're in the midst of painful circumstances. What I've come to understand through my journey is that Universal Intelligence is always guiding us toward remembering our true nature, even when the path includes difficult passages. Sometimes we're simply too stubborn for our good, holding tightly to identities, relationships, beliefs, or circumstances that no longer serve our highest evolution. The Universe loves us too much to let us remain stuck, so it creates conditions that, though challenging, ultimately lead to greater awakening.

I remember sitting on the steps of my home after a devastating breakup, tears streaming down my face as I stared at the moon and asked, "Why me? Why this? Why now?" I couldn't hear the answer then, but years later I understood: that shattering was necessary for me to rebuild myself from the soul outward rather than from external definitions inward. That dark night initiated me into the depths of compassion and spiritual understanding I couldn't have accessed any other way.

Now I can sit with others in their darkest moments with genuine presence and understanding because I've navigated those territories myself.

This is the beautiful paradox of the spiritual journey - our wounds, when approached with consciousness, become the very gateways to our greatest gifts. The places where we've been broken become the places where the most light can enter and eventually shine through us to others. I've witnessed this pattern in thousands of clients and students over the years. The specific circumstances differ, but the essential process remains the same: what appears to be a breakdown is a breakthrough when we bring awareness to it.

So if you're currently moving through a challenging passage, please know this: you are not being punished. You are not failing. You are not lost, though it may feel that way. You are being initiated into greater depths of your light through the only pathway that can create genuine transformation - direct experience integrated with conscious awareness.

Trust the process even when you cannot see where it's leading. The Universe is infinitely wiser than our limited human perspective.

Becoming a channel of light begins with establishing a consistent connection to the energy of God, the Universe, Source, or Spirit - that vast intelligence and love that underlies all existence. This connection isn't something you need to create; it already exists within you as your very essence. Your task is simply to clear away the internal obstacles that prevent you from experiencing it consciously and allowing it to flow through you unimpeded.

My daily meditation practice has been the foundation for deepening this connection over the decades. When I sit in silence, allowing my thoughts to settle like snow in a snow globe, I gradually become aware of a presence that is both within and beyond me—a field of consciousness that feels like home. This presence doesn't speak in ordinary language but communicates through intuitive knowing, expanded awareness, and a profound sense of being held in love. From this connection flows the guidance, healing energy, and creative inspiration that I can then channel into my work and relationships.

You don't need hours of meditation to begin experiencing this connection. Even five minutes of silent sitting each day begins to thin the veil between your ordinary awareness and this deeper dimension of being. As this practice deepens, you may experience it as a tangible current of energy, a quality of luminosity, or simply a profound silence that feels mysteriously alive and intelligent. The specific form matters less than the direct experience itself, which will be unique to you.

While formal meditation creates a foundation, I've learned to strengthen my connection to Source throughout the day through mindful awareness. This involves bringing full attention to ordinary moments and experiencing them directly, rather than through the filter of habitual thinking. When washing dishes, I feel the sensation of water on my hands. When walking outside, I sense the air against my skin and the ground beneath my feet. These simple practices anchor me in the present moment, which is where the energy of God, the Universe, Source, or Spirit is always available.

Your breath serves as a bridge between unconscious bodily processes and conscious awareness. By bringing attention to your breath, following its natural rhythm without trying to control it, you create an entry point for higher frequencies to enter your field. This can be done anywhere, anytime, making it an accessible way to realign with Source energy throughout your day.

For many people, including myself, nature provides the most tangible experience of a connection to the Source. Something about being in natural settings - whether forest, ocean, mountain, or desert - seems to thin the barriers between ordinary perception and spiritual awareness. I make regular time in nature a priority, even if it's just sitting under a tree in a city park. These moments of connection with the natural world renew my energy and help me channel my thoughts more effectively than almost anything else.

As your connection with a higher power, God, the Universe, Source, or Spirit deepens, you'll likely discover, as I have, that staying grounded becomes increasingly important. Grounding means maintaining a strong energetic connection with the Earth while simultaneously opening to higher frequencies. Without this balance, you might experience scattered energy, difficulty focusing, emotional instability, or health challenges.

I start each day by visualizing roots extending from my body into the Earth's core, drawing up stabilizing energy before opening to higher connections. This simple practice has prevented many of the "spaciness" problems that can come with expanding consciousness.

Connecting directly to God, the Universe, Source, or Spirit is the purest and highest form of channeling available to us. While we can certainly connect with various spiritual guides and our own Higher Self, there's something profoundly powerful about opening ourselves to receive directly from the ultimate divine intelligence that underlies all creation.

This direct connection provides the clearest and most unfiltered guidance, the purest frequency of love, and the most comprehensive understanding available to us. When we open ourselves to this primary connection, we access the highest wisdom and most transformative energy possible. This doesn't mean other connections aren't valuable - they certainly are - but connecting directly with the divine offers a particularly pristine quality of transmission.

Your Higher Self plays a crucial role in this process, often serving as a bridge that helps you interpret and integrate divine wisdom in a way your human consciousness can understand. But ultimately, I've found that opening directly to God, the Universe, Source, or Spirit creates the most profound transformation.

I access this direct divine connection through surrendered presence - creating inner stillness, releasing expectations about how guidance should come, and opening with childlike receptivity to whatever wisdom wishes to flow through. Sometimes I simply ask, "Divine Source, what would you have me know right now?" Then I wait in alert receptivity, noticing what arises - whether as intuitive knowing, mental images, physical sensations, or what feels like direct transmission of understanding.

The quality of this communication differs markedly from ordinary mind activity. It feels expansive rather than contracted, liberating rather than limiting. It often brings unexpected perspectives rather than confirming what I already believe. And it invariably carries a frequency of love that feels distinctly different from my everyday emotional states.

With trust and time, you naturally begin to align with higher vibrational frequencies. Vibration refers to the rate at which energy oscillates, with higher frequencies generally associated with states like love, joy, peace, and clarity, while lower frequencies correspond to fear, anger, shame, and confusion. Your vibration results from many factors - your thoughts, emotions, relationships, environment, physical health, and spiritual practices all contribute to your overall energetic signature.

I maintain my vibrational alignment through daily practices that have become as natural as breathing - meditation, time in nature, conscious movement, creative expression, energy clearing techniques, and mindful awareness of my thoughts and emotions. This isn't about achieving perfect vibrational purity, which isn't realistic as an embodied human. It's about processing lower-frequency emotions consciously when they arise rather than getting stuck in them, and intentionally cultivating states that align with higher frequencies.

You may feel called to channel this energy specifically for healing purposes. I discovered my healing abilities gradually, first noticing that people often reported feeling better just from being in my presence, then experiencing spontaneous energy flowing through my hands when someone was in distress. Eventually, I developed these natural capacities through formal training in various healing modalities, but the foundation was always the same: temporarily setting aside my personal will and agenda to serve as a clear conduit for healing frequencies flowing directly from God, the Universe, Source, or Spirit.

Whether you feel drawn to formal healing work or not, your presence itself becomes increasingly healing as you develop as a channel of light. The clear, coherent field you generate affects everyone you encounter, often in ways neither you nor they consciously recognize.

Without trying to "do" anything, your mere presence catalyzes shifts in others' energy systems that support their wellbeing and awakening. This effortless transmission represents one of the most profound aspects of being a channel of light - your being becomes as important as your doing.

This natural evolution toward service and compassion marks the maturing channel of light. What might begin as an interest in developing personal spiritual gifts gradually transforms into a genuine concern for collective wellbeing and a desire to be of service. I've experienced this shift in my journey - from initial focus on developing abilities to increasing joy in supporting others' awakening. This transition from a self-focused to an other-focused orientation doesn't happen through forced altruism, but emerges naturally as you recognize the fundamental interconnection of all beings.

Compassion - the ability to feel with others, coupled with the desire to alleviate suffering - serves as both a pathway for light transmission and an outcome of this transmission. As you channel higher frequencies, your heart naturally opens to greater compassion for the struggles and pain of others. Simultaneously, this compassion creates an open channel through which healing light can flow more abundantly. The relationship is reciprocal, with each quality enhancing the other in an upward spiral of expanding consciousness.

Closely related to compassion is empathy - the capacity to sense and understand another's emotions as if they were your own. As a channel of light, you'll likely find your natural empathy deepening and becoming more refined. This isn't about taking on others' emotions in ways that drain you (which would be unhealthy emotional absorption), but rather about developing the ability to temporarily step into another person's experience while maintaining your energetic integrity.

True empathy is a profound gift that allows you to connect with others at a soul level. It creates bridges of understanding across differences and dissolves the illusion of separation that causes so much suffering in our world. When you empathetically feel with another, you're experiencing the fundamental oneness that underlies our apparent individuality—a direct knowing of our shared divine essence.

You may notice your empathic abilities becoming more discerning. You'll likely develop the capacity to distinguish between different types of emotions and their sources, recognizing when you're picking up someone else's unexpressed feelings versus experiencing your response. This refined empathy becomes an invaluable tool for healing work of all kinds, whether you're formally working as a healer or simply bringing presence to everyday relationships.

The dance between empathy and boundaries becomes crucial as your channel opens more fully. Without proper energetic boundaries, empathic abilities can lead to overwhelm, confusion, and depletion. I've learned to maintain a strong, energetic field that allows me to feel with others without absorbing their energies. This balanced empathy - feeling connected to others while remaining grounded in my center - creates the ideal conditions for acting as a clear channel for divine light and love.

Authentic service as a channel of light doesn't require dramatic outer changes or grand humanitarian gestures, though these may sometimes emerge from your unique path. Often, the most powerful service comes through bringing higher consciousness to ordinary interactions and responsibilities. I've witnessed countless examples of light channels in every field and walk of life - nurses whose presence brings calm to anxious patients, teachers who see and nurture the unique gifts in each student, business leaders who bring integrity and compassion to organizational decisions, parents who raise children with presence and awareness, artists who create from aligned consciousness.

Be sure to maintain balance and proper self-care. I learned this lesson the hard way, experiencing periods of depletion and burnout before understanding that clear boundaries and consistent self-nurturing aren't selfish but essential for sustainable light transmission. The more energy you're capable of channeling, the more crucial these practices become. Just as electrical systems require proper insulation and grounding to safely conduct power, your energy system needs appropriate maintenance to channel higher frequencies effectively.

My self-care regimen includes lots of sleep, nourishing food, regular movement, time in nature, creative expression, meaningful connections, energy-clearing practices, and daily meditation. I've learned to pay attention to my unique needs, which differ from what works for others and change as my channel develops. I encourage you to develop an honest attunement to what genuinely supports your wellbeing, rather than following prescribed formulas or pushing beyond your true capacity.

Healthy boundaries prevent energy drain that would compromise channel clarity. This includes being selective about where, when, and how you offer your gifts; maintaining energetic protection during interactions with others; clearly distinguishing between your energy and others'; and ensuring appropriate exchange for services rather than giving from depletion. I've discovered that strong boundaries actually enhance rather than limit my capacity to serve, creating sustainable conditions for light transmission.

You may discover an increasing ability to consciously manifest experiences aligned with your soul's purpose. I've witnessed this phenomenon throughout my journey - when I'm aligned with my authentic path, the external circumstances that support my expression tend to materialize more readily, often in unexpected ways. This isn't about manipulating reality through spiritual techniques but rather about partnering with universal intelligence to express your unique gifts most effectively.

Living with conscious purpose dramatically expands your capacity as a channel. By "conscious purpose," I mean making choices with full awareness of your deepest intentions and highest values, rather than operating on autopilot. It's about regularly checking in with God, the Universe, Source, or Spirit to ensure your actions align with divine wisdom rather than ego desires. When you connect your daily activities to the larger mission that the divine has for your life, you access energy far beyond what's available through personal will alone.

This conscious alignment with Source doesn't necessarily make your path easier in conventional terms - it may lead you through challenges that catalyze necessary growth - but it fills your life with meaning and provides renewable energy for your journey. I've found that even difficult passages feel purposeful rather than merely painful when I understand how they connect to the divine plan unfolding through my life.

The impact of becoming a channel of light extends far beyond what you can personally observe or measure. Like dropping a stone into water, your presence creates ripples that affect the entire field of consciousness. Someone who experiences your channeled light might later transmit that frequency to others who never meet you directly. A brief interaction where you embody presence might catalyze a significant shift in someone's life path. A situation where you channel compassion might heal trauma that would otherwise perpetuate cycles of suffering.

This ripple effect represents the heart of my mission - lighting up other channels of light who will, in turn, illuminate others in an ever-expanding wave of awakening. I envision a world where millions of conscious light channels create a network of higher frequency that elevates our entire planetary field. This isn't naive idealism but practical spiritual vision. Throughout history, relatively small numbers of aligned individuals have catalyzed significant shifts in human consciousness. Today, as more people awaken to their role as channels of light, we're witnessing an unprecedented elevation in collective frequency.

As I look at our world with all its challenges and possibilities, I feel tremendous hope. Not because I ignore the very real problems we face, but because I've witnessed the extraordinary power of awakened consciousness to transform seemingly impossible situations. Every time one person remembers their true nature as a channel of light and begins expressing this remembrance through their unique gifts and presence, our collective potential expands.

This is how transformation happens - not primarily through external revolution but through internal remembrance that naturally manifests as evolved external expression.

I want to congratulate you on the path you've walked thus far.

Whether you're just beginning to explore these concepts or have been consciously developing as a channel of light for decades, the very fact that you're reading these words indicates your soul's readiness for this journey. Every experience you've had - the joys and sorrows, achievements and failures, connections and losses - has prepared you for this moment of deeper awakening to your true nature and purpose.

Remember that the Universe doesn't punish us - it loves us too much for that. What appears as punishment from our limited perspective is actually an invitation to remember more of who we truly are. Sometimes we resist this invitation, holding tightly to familiar patterns even when they cause suffering. We are, indeed, often too stubborn for our own good! But Universal Intelligence is infinitely patient, continuing to create conditions that support our eventual awakening, no matter how many detours we take along the way.

The journey of becoming a channel of light will continue throughout your lifetime, with each phase bringing new depths, challenges, and opportunities for service. What begins as a conscious effort gradually becomes your natural state of being. The boundaries between spiritual practice and ordinary life dissolve as you recognize every moment as an opportunity to channel light. Your presence itself becomes your greatest gift to the world - a living transmission of the peace, love, joy, and wisdom that constitute your true nature.

As we conclude our time together in these pages, I want to leave you with this essential truth: you are already a channel of light by your very nature. Your journey isn't about becoming something you're not but rather clearing away what obscures who you've always been. The practices, understandings, and experiences we've explored together simply help reveal and strengthen what already exists within you - your inherent connection to God, the Universe, Source, or Spirit, and your capacity to transmit this connection through your unique human expression.

The world needs your light now more than ever. Not a perfect, transcendent light that denies human complexity, but the authentic light that shines through your whole being - your joy and sorrow, your strengths and vulnerabilities, your knowledge and not-knowing. As you embrace your role as a channel of light here on Earth, you join countless others in the most important work of our time - the elevation of consciousness that makes possible a more compassionate, just, and beautiful world for all beings.

This happens through conscious breath, kind words, present attention, compassionate touch, creative expression, principled action, and silent presence. It happens through you, just as you are, when you choose to align with the highest light you can access in any given moment. This is what it means to become a channel of light here on Earth - to remember your true nature and allow it to shine through the unique vessel of your human life.

I see your light, even if you're still learning to recognize it fully yourself. And I'm profoundly grateful for the privilege of accompanying you on this journey, even for these few pages.

May your channel grow ever clearer, and may your light shine ever brighter, illuminating not only your own path but the paths of all whose lives you touch.

With deepest love and gratitude,
Sonya

Continuing Your Journey: Resources and Practices

Now that we've completed our exploration of becoming a channel of light, I'd like to offer you some practical resources to support your ongoing journey. The path of spiritual development doesn't end with the final page of this book - it continues to unfold throughout your lifetime, with each day bringing new opportunities to refine your channel and express your light more fully in the world.

Affirmations for Channels of Light

One of the most powerful ways to reinforce your development as a channel of light is through the conscious use of affirmations. These statements, when spoken with intention and feeling, help reprogram subconscious patterns and strengthen your energetic alignment with higher frequencies. I've created the following affirmations specifically to support the practices and principles we've explored throughout this book. I recommend selecting a few that particularly resonate with your current needs and working with them daily for at least 21 days.
I am a channel of divine light and healing energy.

- My intuition grows stronger each day.
- I trust the wisdom of my higher self.
- I am connected to the infinite source of universal energy.
- My body is a Golden Light for spiritual growth.
- I release all that no longer serves my highest good.
- I am worthy of love, abundance, and spiritual connection.
- My energy field is strong, clear, and protected.
- I honor the divine in myself and others.
- I am open to receiving guidance from my spirit guides.
- Each challenge I face is an opportunity for spiritual growth.
- I radiate love and compassion to all beings.
- My chakras are balanced and flowing with vibrant energy.
- I am grounded in my body and connected to the Earth.
- I trust in the perfect unfolding of my spiritual journey.
- I am a powerful co-creator with the Universe.
- My consciousness expands with each passing day.
- I embrace my unique gifts and purpose.
- I am at peace with my past and excited for my future.
- Divine wisdom flows through me effortlessly.
- I am aligned with my highest truth.
- I release fear and embrace love.
- My heart is open to give and receive love freely.
- I am a beacon of light in this world.
- I trust my ability to discern truth and wisdom.
- I am worthy of spiritual knowledge and growth.
- My intuitive abilities strengthen with each passing day.
- I am in tune with the rhythms of nature and the cosmos.
- I honor my body as a temple of spiritual energy.
- I am grateful for the spiritual lessons in every experience.
- I am becoming more aware and conscious each day.
- I release limiting beliefs and embrace infinite possibilities.
- I am connected to the wisdom of my ancestors.
- My energy field is a sanctuary of peace and healing.

- I trust in the divine timing of my spiritual awakening.
- I am open to miracles and synchronicities in my life.
- I am a clear channel for divine inspiration and creativity.
- I release the need to control and surrender to divine flow.
- I am worthy of spiritual experiences and divine connection.
- My spiritual practice deepens with each passing day.
- I am at peace with the mystery of existence.
- I trust my inner guidance system implicitly.
- I am aligned with my soul's highest purpose.
- I radiate healing energy to myself and others.
- I am open to receiving abundance in all forms.
- My consciousness is expanding beyond limiting beliefs.
- I am a bridge between the physical and spiritual realms.
- I release energetic attachments that no longer serve me.
- I am in harmony with the universal flow of energy.
- I trust in the wisdom of my body and energy field.
- I am open to receiving messages from the Universe.
- My spiritual gifts unfold naturally and effortlessly.
- I am deserving of spiritual growth and enlightenment.
- I release the past and embrace the present moment.
- I am attuned to the subtle energies around me.
- My intuition guides me to my highest good.
- I am a vessel for divine love and healing.
- I trust in the journey of my soul's evolution.
- I am open to experiencing higher states of consciousness.
- My energy field is cleansed and renewed each day.
- I am connected to the infinite wisdom of the Akashic Records.
- I release doubt and embrace faith in my spiritual path.
- I am worthy of divine protection and guidance.
- My spiritual practice brings me peace and clarity.
- I am aligned with the highest vibrations of love and light.
- I trust in the unseen forces supporting my journey.
- I am open to receiving healing on all levels of my being.

- My consciousness expands beyond the limitations of the physical world.
- I am a conduit for divine healing energy.
- I release resistance and surrender to divine will.
- I am in tune with the cosmic rhythms of the Universe.
- My spiritual awareness grows stronger each day.
- I trust in the divine plan for my life.
- I am open to receiving cosmic wisdom and knowledge.
- My energy field is a beacon of light and healing.
- I release old patterns and embrace new ways of being.
- I am worthy of spiritual communion and divine experiences.
- My intuition guides me to my highest truth.
- I am aligned with the infinite potential of the Universe.
- I trust in the process of my spiritual unfoldment.
- I am open to channeling divine wisdom and energy.
- My consciousness transcends time and space.
- I release fear of the unknown and embrace spiritual growth.
- I am a clear channel for divine love and wisdom.
- My spiritual journey is unfolding perfectly.
- I trust in the innate wisdom of my soul.
- I am open to experiencing the magic of the Universe.
- I am, in every moment, a being of infinite light and love.

For maximum benefit, speak these affirmations aloud while feeling their truth in your body. You might also write them in a journal, meditate on them, or create visual reminders of those that particularly resonate with your current phase of development.

Working with Sonya Directly

While books provide valuable knowledge and guidance, direct personal work often accelerates spiritual development in ways that written information alone cannot achieve. The unique energies, blockages, and gifts that compose your individual channel sometimes require personalized attention to fully activate and refine.

If you feel called to deepen your development as a channel of light through more direct guidance and energetic support, I offer several pathways for working together:

1:1 Intuitive Guidance + Psychic Healing Sessions

These one-on-one sessions combine intuitive readings with energy healing to provide personalized support for your development as a channel of light. During these sessions, I use my psychic abilities to identify energetic blockages, karmic patterns, and spiritual gifts in your energy field, then provide targeted healing to help you move forward on your path. I also connect directly with your highest frequency spirit team so that we can channel specific information needed for your path forward. These sessions are particularly valuable for:

- Clearing energetic blockages that prevent full expression of your channel
- Identifying, developing and learning to use your unique spiritual gifts and purpose
- Healing past trauma that affects your current energy field
- Receiving specific guidance about your spiritual path and purpose
- Addressing challenging situations with higher perspective

Group Mentorship Programs

For ongoing support and development in community with like-minded souls, I offer two levels of group membership mentorship:

- **Higher Frequency** - Meeting twice monthly, this group provides regular connection, energy work, and teaching to support your consistent growth as a channel of light. Members receive guidance, participate in group energy healing, and learn practical techniques for spiritual development in daily life.

- **Quantum Leap** - This more intensive option includes four monthly sessions for those ready to accelerate their development as channels of light. With twice the connection and support of Higher Frequency, Quantum Leap members experience deeper transformation and more rapid clearing of obstacles to their spiritual expression.

Both membership options create powerful group fields that amplify individual development while providing the support and accountability that helps maintain consistent practice.

Quantum Leader™ Private Mentorship

This exclusive one-on-one mentorship program is designed for established or emerging leaders who wish to integrate spiritual awareness with their professional roles and responsibilities.

Whether you're leading an organization, building a conscious business, or seeking to influence your professional environment with higher consciousness, this program provides personalized guidance for:

- Developing intuitive decision-making in professional contexts
- Maintaining energetic boundaries in demanding environments

- Channeling higher guidance for strategic direction
- Creating organizational cultures that support wellbeing and consciousness
- Navigating leadership challenges from a spiritually-grounded perspective

Group Programs and Workshops

Throughout the year, I offer specialized group programs and workshops focused on specific aspects of becoming a channel of light. These include "Mindfulness for Busy Executives," which provides practical approaches to presence and energy management for those in demanding professional roles. These programs combine teaching, practice, and energy work in supportive community settings.

Group work offers the added benefit of community support and the amplified field that forms when multiple people engage in spiritual practice together. Many participants find that certain blockages release more easily in group settings, and connections formed with like-minded seekers provide ongoing support for their spiritual journey.

- Foundations of Quantum Meditation
- Developing Your Intuitive Gifts
- Channeling for Healing and Creativity
- Navigating the Dark Night of the Soul
- Sacred Geometry and Universal Patterns
- Establishing Healthy Spiritual Boundaries
- Practitioner Training Programs (Coming Soon)

For those who feel called to develop professional skills as channels of light for others, I am developing comprehensive training programs that will provide both spiritual development and practical skills for ethical, effective practice. If you're interested in being notified when these programs become available, please visit my website to join the waitlist.

Next Steps

If you feel drawn to any of these opportunities for deepening your development as a channel of light, I invite you to visit my website at https://www.sonyalee.io to learn more about current offerings and to schedule a complimentary consultation. During this initial conversation, we can discuss where you are on your spiritual path, what challenges you're currently facing, and which approach might best support your unique journey.

Whether or not we work together directly, please know that I honor your commitment to developing as a channel of light and trust that you will find the perfect support for your continued evolution. The very fact that you've engaged with this book indicates your readiness for this journey and your soul's alignment with this path of service and transformation.

May your channel continue to clear and strengthen, allowing ever greater light to flow through you into a world that deeply needs your unique gifts. Remember that you don't have to be perfect to make a profound difference - your willingness to show up authentically, with both your light and your humanity fully present, is exactly what makes your contribution so valuable.

Appendix

Glossary of Terms

Akashic Records
A non-physical repository of all knowledge and experiences from all lifetimes, past, present, and future. Often described as a cosmic library, the Akashic Records are believed to contain every thought, word, and action of every living being in the Universe. Accessing these records is said to provide profound insights and guidance.

Ascended Masters
Highly evolved spiritual beings who once lived on Earth and have transcended the cycle of rebirth. They are believed to guide humanity from higher realms. Examples include Jesus, Buddha, Saint Germain, and Kwan Yin. Ascended Masters are often called upon for spiritual guidance and support in healing work.

Astral Projection
The practice of intentionally separating one's consciousness from the physical body, allowing for travel in the astral plane. This out-of-body experience can be used for spiritual exploration, healing, and gaining higher knowledge.

Aura
The electromagnetic energy field that surrounds all living beings. Often

described as a colorful egg-shaped field, the aura reflects a person's physical, emotional, mental, and spiritual state. Aura reading is a skill that allows one to perceive and interpret this energy field.

Chakra

Energy centers in the body that regulate physical, emotional, and spiritual well-being. The seven main chakras are:
1. Root (Muladhara)
2. Sacral (Svadhisthana)
3. Solar Plexus (Manipura)
4. Heart (Anahata)
5. Throat (Vishuddha)
6. Third Eye (Ajna)
7. Crown (Sahasrara)

Each chakra is associated with specific qualities and aspects of human experience.

Channeling

The practice of receiving and transmitting information from non-physical entities, collective consciousnesses, or higher aspects of oneself. Channeling can involve verbal communication, automatic writing, or other forms of expression.

Clairaudience

The psychic ability to hear sounds, words, or music beyond the range of ordinary auditory perception. This "clear hearing" can involve receiving messages from spirits, guides, or higher realms of consciousness.

Clairsentience

The psychic ability to sense or feel energies, emotions, or physical sensations beyond ordinary perception. This "clear feeling" allows one to gather information about people, places, or objects through intuitive sensing.

Clairvoyance
The psychic ability to see images, symbols, or scenes beyond ordinary visual perception. This "clear seeing" can involve perceiving auras, spirit beings, or events past, present, or future.

Dark Night of the Soul
A profound period of spiritual crisis and transformation, often characterized by feelings of despair, loss of meaning, and intense inner turmoil. This phase is seen as a necessary part of spiritual growth, leading to deeper awareness and connection with one's true self.

Ego
In spiritual contexts, the ego refers to the sense of separate self that can hinder spiritual growth. It's often associated with fear, attachment, and resistance to change. Spiritual practices often aim to transcend or integrate the ego for higher awareness.

Energy Healing
A range of therapeutic modalities that work with the body's energy systems to promote physical, emotional, and spiritual well-being. Examples include Reiki, acupuncture, and quantum healing.

Enlightenment
A state of profound spiritual realization and awakening, characterized by a direct experience of ultimate reality or one's true nature. Often described as a dissolution of the ego and a merging with universal consciousness.

Etheric Body
The first or lowest layer of the human energy field, closely mirroring the physical body. It's believed to be the blueprint for the physical body and plays a crucial role in energy healing practices.

Grounding
The practice of connecting one's energy with the Earth's energy, promoting stability, presence, and balance. Grounding techniques are essential in energy work and spiritual practices to maintain a healthy connection between spiritual and physical realities.

Higher Self
The eternal, wise aspect of one's being that exists beyond the ego and personality. Connecting with the Higher Self is often a goal in spiritual practices, as it's believed to offer guidance, wisdom, and a direct link to universal consciousness.

Intuition
An innate ability to understand or know something without conscious reasoning. In spiritual contexts, intuition is often seen as a direct line to higher wisdom and is cultivated as a key tool for personal growth and decision-making.

Karma
The universal law of cause and effect, where one's actions, thoughts, and intentions create corresponding effects in one's life. Karma is often viewed as a tool for soul growth and learning across multiple lifetimes.

Karmic Contract
The universal agreement where a soul agrees to learn spiritual lessons here on earth for the souls evolution and growth.

Kundalini
A powerful spiritual energy believed to lie dormant at the base of the spine. When awakened, Kundalini energy rises through the chakras, potentially leading to profound spiritual experiences and transformation.

Manifestation

The process of bringing thoughts, desires, or intentions into physical reality. Based on the principle that consciousness shapes reality, manifestation practices often involve visualization, affirmation, and alignment with desired outcomes.

Meditation

A practice of focused attention or awareness, often used to cultivate inner peace, clarity, and spiritual insight. There are many forms of meditation, including mindfulness, transcendental, and loving-kindness meditation.

Meridians

In Traditional Chinese Medicine, meridians are energy pathways in the body through which qi (life force energy) flows. Acupuncture and other energy healing modalities work with these meridians to promote health and balance.

Mindfulness

The practice of bringing one's attention to the present moment with openness, curiosity, and non-judgment. Mindfulness is a key aspect of many spiritual and therapeutic approaches, promoting greater awareness and emotional regulation.

Past Life Regression

A therapeutic or spiritual practice that aims to recover memories of past lives through hypnosis or deep meditation. This practice is based on the belief in reincarnation and is often used for healing and personal growth.

Prana

In yoga and Ayurvedic traditions, prana refers to the vital life force energy that permeates all of existence. Practices like pranayama (breath control) aim to increase and balance prana in the body.

Quantum Healing
A healing approach that draws on principles of quantum physics, working with the idea that consciousness can directly influence matter and energy at the quantum level to promote healing and transformation.

Reiki
A Japanese energy healing technique that channels universal life force energy through the practitioner to the recipient. Reiki is used to promote relaxation, reduce stress, and support the body's natural healing processes.

Shadow Work
The process of acknowledging, exploring, and integrating the unconscious aspects of oneself, including repressed emotions, desires, and traits. Shadow work is seen as essential for personal growth and spiritual development.

Shamanism
An ancient spiritual practice that involves entering altered states of consciousness to interact with the spirit world for healing, guidance, and knowledge. Shamanic practices vary across cultures but often involve journeying, ritual, and working with plant medicines.

Soul Retrieval
A shamanic healing practice that aims to recover and reintegrate lost parts of the soul. These soul parts are believed to split off due to trauma or difficult life experiences, and their recovery is thought to bring about healing and wholeness.

Spiritual Awakening
A profound shift in consciousness and perception, often characterized by a greater sense of connection to all of life, increased awareness, and a reevaluation of one's beliefs and values. Spiritual awakenings can be gradual or sudden and often lead to significant life changes.

Third Eye

Associated with the sixth chakra (Ajna), the third eye is considered the center of intuition, insight, and spiritual perception. Opening or activating the third eye is often a goal in spiritual practices, believed to enhance psychic abilities and spiritual awareness.

Vibrational Frequency

The rate at which energy vibrates, often used in spiritual contexts to describe the quality or level of consciousness. Higher vibrational frequencies are associated with positive emotions, health, and spiritual growth.

RECOMMENDED RESOURCES

Website: https://www.sonyalee.io - Visit my official website to learn more about mentorship programs, healing sessions, and other offerings.

Books:
- "The Power of Now" by Eckhart Tolle
- "A New Earth" by Eckhart Tolle
- "The Untethered Soul" by Michael A. Singer
- "The Body Keeps the Score" by Bessel van der Kolk

Documentaries:
- "Inner Worlds, Outer Worlds"
- "The Connected Universe"
- "Heal"

Podcasts:
- "On Being with Krista Tippett"
- "Oprah's Super Soul Conversations"
- "Tara Brach"

Apps:
- Insight Timer (for meditation)
- Calm
- Headspace

GUIDED MEDITATIONS & EXERCISES

Free Energy Cleansing:
- Download your free chakra cleansing meditation here on my website: https://members.sonyalee.io/energyclearing

Grounding Meditation:

- Find a comfortable seated position.
- Close your eyes and take three deep breaths.
- Visualize roots growing from the base of your spine, down through the earth.
- See these roots reaching deep into the core of the Earth.
- Feel yourself anchored and supported by the Earth's energy.
- Sit with this feeling for 5-10 minutes.
- When ready, slowly open your eyes.

Chakra Balancing Exercise:

- Lie down comfortably.
- Starting at your root chakra (base of spine), visualize a red spinning wheel of energy.
- As you breathe, see this wheel becoming balanced and vibrant.
- Move up to the sacral chakra (lower abdomen) and repeat with orange energy.
- Continue through each chakra: solar plexus (yellow), heart (green), throat (blue), third eye (indigo), and crown (violet).

- Spend about a minute on each chakra.
- Finish by visualizing all chakras spinning in harmony.

Loving-Kindness Meditation:

- Sit comfortably and close your eyes.
- Bring to mind someone you love deeply.
- Silently repeat: "May you be happy. May you be healthy. May you be safe. May you live with ease."
- Now direct these wishes to yourself.
- Extend them to a neutral person, then to someone you find difficult.
- Finally, send these wishes to all beings everywhere.
- Practice for 10-15 minutes.

Energy Clearing Visualization:

- Stand with your eyes closed.
- Visualize a bright white light above your head.
- See this light pouring down over you, cleansing your energy field.
- As the light moves down your body, see it washing away any dark or stagnant energy.
- When the light reaches your feet, see it grounding into the Earth.
- Take a deep breath and open your eyes.

Gratitude Journal Exercise:

- Each night before bed, write down three things you're grateful for.
- They can be as small as going on a short walk, or drinking a glass of water. Or as big as accomplishing a lifetime goal.
- Big or small, celebrate all the wins.
- Reflect on why you're grateful for each item.
- Repeat this for 21 days.
- Notice how this practice affects your mood and outlook over time.

BONUS: Experience the Power of a Quantum Meditation

Begin by finding a comfortable position, either sitting or lying down. Close your eyes and take a few deep breaths, allowing your body to relax with each exhale. Let go of any tension or thoughts about your day. You are entering a space of peace and exploration.

Now, bring your awareness to your inner energy and body. Feel the life force pulsing within you. Notice the subtle sensations in your fingers, your toes, your limbs. Become aware of the energy flowing through your entire being.

As you continue to breathe deeply and steadily, imagine a bright, radiant light beginning to form in your heart chakra. This light is warm, comforting, and full of love. It grows brighter with each breath, expanding within your chest.

Now, visualize this light beginning to flow downward from your heart. It moves slowly, like a golden river, down through your solar plexus, into your sacral chakra, and finally reaching your root chakra at the base of your spine.

Feel the warmth and energy of this light as it pools in your root chakra. Take a moment to experience the grounding and stability it brings.

Now, this river of light begins to flow upward. It moves back through your sacral chakra, energizing and balancing as it goes. It passes through your solar plexus, empowering your sense of self. The light flows back into your heart chakra, expanding and intensifying.

The light continues its upward journey, moving into your throat chakra, illuminating your voice and truth. It flows further, into your third eye chakra, awakening your inner vision and intuition.

Finally, the light reaches your crown chakra at the top of your head. Feel it pooling here, growing brighter and more intense.

Now, visualize this light beginning to stream out of your crown chakra, creating a pillar of light that extends upward. This beam of light carries your consciousness up, up through the ceiling, through the sky, beyond the clouds.

You're moving faster now, passing through the layers of the atmosphere. You see the curve of the Earth below you as you continue to ascend.

Now, you find yourself suspended in the vast darkness of the Universe. Stars twinkle around you in every direction. Galaxies swirl in the distance. Take a moment to marvel at the beauty and vastness of the cosmos.

As you float here in this cosmic space, allow yourself to explore. Perhaps you feel drawn to a particular star or planet. Maybe you sense a presence nearby. Be open to whatever experiences come to you.

Don't be afraid. You are safe here, held in the loving embrace of the Universe. If any beings or energies come forward to greet you, know that they are here for your highest good.

This is a time for receiving. If you have any questions, allow them to form in your mind. Listen for the answers that may come as words, images, or feelings. Your spirit team is here with you, ready to offer guidance, healing, and upgrades to your energy.

Take your time in this space. Receive what is offered to you. Allow the cosmic energies to wash over and through you, cleansing, rejuvenating, and elevating your vibration.

[Pause for a few minutes of silence]

Now, it's time to begin your journey back. Visualize yourself gently floating downward, back towards Earth. You pass through the starry expanse, re-entering Earth's atmosphere.

You see the planet growing larger beneath you, continents and oceans coming into view. You float down towards your country, your region, your city.

Now you see your neighborhood, your street, your home. Gently, you descend back into your room, back to your physical body.

As you settle back into your body, feel the energy from your cosmic journey flowing down from your crown chakra. It moves through each of your chakras - third eye, throat, heart, solar plexus, sacral - finally reaching your root chakra.

From the root, feel this energy returning to your heart. It settles here, a warm, glowing ball of light and cosmic wisdom.

Take a few deep breaths, allowing this energy to integrate fully into your being. Feel it spreading to every cell of your body, rejuvenating and enlightening.

When you're ready, begin to wiggle your fingers and toes. Take a deeper breath and slowly open your eyes.

You are now fully back in your body, grounded and present, yet carrying within you the light and wisdom of your cosmic journey. Take a moment to stretch and reflect on your experience, knowing you can return to this cosmic space whenever you need guidance or renewal.

Final notes: Remember, consistent practice is key to developing your spiritual abilities and maintaining energetic health. Even a few minutes of daily practice can make a significant difference in your overall well-being and spiritual growth.

If you find yourself forgetting what to do, revisit the earlier chapters where we talk about integrating your spirituality into daily life.

ACKNOWLEDGMENTS

There are so many people that I'd like to thank - but the most important of all is my poh poh (maternal grandmother) and yeh yeh (maternal grandfather), ma ma (paternal grandmother) and gong gong (paternal grandfather) who encouraged me from behind the veil in their afterlife, to tell/ask/demand that I follow in our family lineage and share our gifts with the world. Thank you for being my guiding light and inspiration.

To my beloved friends who have stood by me through every triumph and tribulation - Janelle, Jennifer, Tamara, Rudy, Christina R., Emidio, Alison, Sheena, Sue, Robert, Bridget, Nimesh, Brittney, Kaye, Denton, Sherri, David, Jerry, Matthew B., Amy, Angela, TBird, Jessie, Katie, Trace, Ivette, Tyrone, Malcolm, Preeti, Victor, BethAnne, Matthew M., Lori, Bill, Jorge, Juliana, Markus, Ryan, Joseph, Idin, Mary, Kylie, Christina S. and so many more friends to name - your unwavering love and support have been my anchor. Thank you for reminding me of who I truly am when I needed it most. This journey would have been impossible without your presence in my life.

To my beloved four-legged babies who have sat by me through every joy and frustration and quietly watched over and protected me from the multiverse - Sushi, Mickey, Sabi, Kaeli, Misty, Spike, Monster, Minxie, and my current babies, Ocean Alo, Bodhi Ama, and Baby Button.

To my spirit guides and team - Zee, the collective of over a hundred of energetic beings from the Cosmic Realms, as well as Jesus, Mother Mary, Mary Magdalene, Buddha, Kwan Yin, Archangel Michael, Raphael, Metatron, Ophanim, God, Spirit, Source, Creator and of course, the Universe. You are all pretty cool.

To Janelle, for literally saving my life and being there for me when I hit rock bottom. Without you, I would not exist today. Thank you for being my rock and safe place to call 'home'.

To Tamara and Rudy, for witnessing my awakening and allowing me to 'lose my lunch' while you both persisted in my well-being and growth. Without you, this work would never have happened.

To Jennifer, my forever business partner, my soul sister - thank you for holding me to such a high standard that I could not even fathom that I would have ever landed on my own two feet doing what I do today. I'm sorry I was the biggest diva (as your UX expert), but I love my spiritual work more than I do pixels! Xo

To Alison, the owner of the Zen Den in Huntington Beach, I owe you a million thanks for forcing and encouraging me to start teaching quantum meditation at your yoga studio. Had you not put me on the spot and encouraged me to just start, I would not be doing what I do today. You saw the light within me and held me accountable. I love you, friend.

To my Higher Frequency, Quantum Leap, and Quantum Leader™ community - thank you for lighting up my soul and being the bright channels of light here in this world. You continue to inspire and guide me higher and forward.

To my Idyllwild community - though I know not everyone may resonate with my path, this small mountain town has become my sanctuary. Having grown up in a small northern California town, finding this place has been like returning home. Thank you, Rev. Shelly - you were the only person I knew here. Thank you for introducing me to a few people to get me started and for believing in me. To Amelia and Jim for being so warm and welcoming and letting me sit with you for coffee and donuts! To my former landlord, Chris, who gave me a chance to call Idyllwild home, and my current landlords, Bob and Heather. I'm deeply grateful to you and all who have welcomed me into your hearts, homes, and community.

To my blood relatives with whom I have no relationship today, thank you for playing a very difficult role in my life and pushing me to my limits so I could remember who I am today.

And to everyone who has crossed my path - whether briefly or for seasons of my life, whether our encounters were challenging or joyful - I thank you.

Each of you has played an essential role in shaping who I am today. The difficult moments stretched me toward growth, while the beautiful ones nourished my spirit. In ways you may never know, you've contributed to the light I now channel into the world.

This book is a testament to the interconnected web of relationships that transforms us all. May it serve as a beacon for those seeking to recognize their own light, just as each of you has helped illuminate mine.

Xoxo, Sonya

ABOUT THE AUTHOR

Sonya Lee stands at the rare intersection of ancient spiritual wisdom and modern business acumen - a true bridge between worlds. Descended from a prestigious lineage of healers and shamans on both sides of her family, Sonya's spiritual gifts emerged at a remarkably young age. By eight years old, she was already teaching meditation classes before being raised in a Buddhist monastery, laying the foundation for her extraordinary path as a channel of light.

Her journey took an unexpected turn when she entered the corporate world, where she spent 25 years as an award-winning designer turned highly sought-after change management consultant. During this time, Sonya transformed major global companies including Warner Bros, Disney, MGM, Cisco, AT&T, TrueCar, and Adobe - guiding them through complex digital evolutions. This extensive experience in high-pressure corporate environments gave her a profound understanding of the practical challenges faced by today's leaders.

What sets Sonya apart is not just her business expertise or spiritual lineage but the revelation that came later in her journey— the discovery of her direct ancestral connection to a Shang

Dynasty priestess (c. 1600 BCE). This ancient shamanic heritage explains her natural abilities in energy healing, clairvoyance, and channeling, gifts that emerged without formal training yet mirror those of her ancestors from millennia past.

Today, Sonya creates a sacred, confidential space for CEOs, celebrities, high-achievers and visionary leaders seeking authentic spiritual guidance without the noise of commercialized spirituality. Her clients - many among the most influential figures in entertainment, technology, and business - trust her because she understands both the unique pressures of high-profile positions and the timeless truths of spiritual wisdom.

Sonya's approach is refreshingly grounded yet profoundly transformative. She brings the analytical precision of her corporate background together with the intuitive depth of her spiritual lineage, offering guidance that honors both external success and internal awakening. Through one-on-one work, small group experiences, and her writings, she helps others recognize and develop their own unique gifts as channels of light.

In a world where true spiritual guidance is increasingly rare, Sonya Lee stands as a beacon of authentic wisdom - a master practitioner who bridges ancient traditions with contemporary challenges, helping today's leaders navigate both the visible and invisible dimensions of their lives with clarity, purpose, and power.

To learn more about Sonya, visit https://www.sonyalee.io or follow her on Instagram at SonyaLeeOfficial.

www.ingramcontent.com/pod-product-compliance
Lightning Source LLC
Chambersburg PA
CBHW030453100526
44580CB00009B/120/J